To Ja
Hope y

Bob Eastley
09/20/16

THE DAILY GRIPE

ROBERT EASTLEY

Illustrations: Anna Cassata
Back photo: Bill Bitzinger

Green Ivy Publishing
1 Lincoln Centre
18W140 Butterfield Road
Suite 1500
Oakbrook Terrace IL 60181-4843
www.greenivybooks.com

ISBN: 978-1-945379-58-1

The Daily Gripe

Acknowledgments

I'd like to thank some very special people for providing inspiration and encouraging me to follow through with this thing. At the top of the list are my wife, Jan, and my daughters, Amy and Sarah. I'd also like to thank the Big Rapids gang, as well as lots of dear friends and family scattered across the country and even in the Czech Republic. You know who you are, and your love and friendship means the world to me. Also, thanks to the Big Rapids Pioneer for giving me an opportunity.

Dedication

This book is dedicated to Jack and Alex, the two coolest kids on the planet.

Chapter 1

The Skinny on Food

A hundred years ago, food was boring and basic. You chowed down a big meal of meat and potatoes and headed out to work in the fields. These days, we want our cuisine to be fast and fun. It has to be long on presentation, short on calories, nutritious, delicious, and completely devoid of fat grams. Not likely.

All About Fast Food

Like most of you, I eat my fair share of fast food. A couple of buddies and I love to make semiannual pilgrimages to Colorado, Wyoming, and other wild-west destinations to do the skiing and trout fishing thing. And, while traveling, we live almost exclusively on three of the four basic food groups (caffeine, cholesterol, sugar, and alcohol). The plan is to get in the car, set the cruise control on Warp 3, drive for 30 hours, and stop only for gas and burgers to go.

It was on one of these cross-country excursions that I encountered Leonard the Incredibly Bad Cashier.

OK, we all have to work somewhere, but different people have different aptitudes. Leonard should have been an apprentice fry guy. It really bothers me when management assigns a cash register to a person who doesn't quite grasp the whole numbers thing.

Anyhow, I met Leonard somewhere in western Nebraska. When I came into that restaurant I was operating on little or no sleep, with plenty of caffeine and ibuprofen coursing through my veins, hands shaking, a stiff neck, and really needing a hot shower. Well, you get the picture. Leonard stood there smiling, and I, because I was too tired to be creative, ordered what I always order in those places: a burger, large fries, and large Coke.

So far, so good. It should have been easy. After all, I'd only ordered three things. Heck, they only sold eight things.

(This was before the days of salads and baked potatoes and stuff like that.) No matter; this is when Leonard downshifted into low.

He stared at his computer, appearing to study it carefully. His face brightened, and he turned and walked slowly to a collection of greasy looking fries that appeared to have been tanning themselves for some time under the heat lamp. He returned with the fries, placed them on the tray, and paused again to study the computer, appearing somewhat confused. Could he have forgotten what I ordered?

After what seemed an eternity, he again about-faced and headed (even more slowly) for the burger bin. I was overcome by an urge to say, "Hey, just a burger, fries, and a Coke," but I held my tongue, not wanting to disturb his rhythm. He returned with the burger, again studied the computer, and repeated the process with the Coke. I swear that if he'd gone any slower, he'd have been in danger of getting painted.

Finally, with all the food safely delivered, he rang it up and said, "That'll be $3.08." I handed him a five-dollar bill and a quarter, and a peculiar thing happened: His eyes literally glazed over. I haven't seen that look since my calculus teacher leered out at us and tried to explain triple integration. Leonard looked at the money, then at the cash register, then again at the money, and then he looked at me, as though pleading for mercy.

Sensing my hostility, he put the money in the till and took his best shot. He produced a five, a one, and seven cents in change (don't ask me how he arrived at this), and placed them in my hand, a nervous smile on his lips, his eyes begging for approval. I should have taken the money and walked, but I'm just too nice a guy.

In a small effort at humor, I offered to trade him the five spot for a one-dollar bill and 10 cents. I might as well have been reading the Old Testament to him in the original Hebrew, and he looked at me suspiciously, his eyes glazing over even more.

Finally, we decided to call in reinforcements, and the manager came over and straightened things out. Forty-five minutes after arriving, we were finally on the road again with cold fries and the correct change. About a hundred miles west of there we had to stop and wait for over an hour while the Highway Patrol cleaned up a rollover accident that had blocked the freeway. I couldn't help thinking that we owed this little inconvenience to my new pal back at the restaurant.

I've been back through that area several times in recent years, but I don't know what became of fast Leonard, the random change maker. I suppose he went on to become a banker—or maybe a calculus teacher.

Fast-Food Seminars

In my opinion, the most important qualities of *fast*-food restaurants are that they're supposed to be *fast*—and inexpensive. If the food is reasonably tasty and can be eaten with one hand in heavy traffic, it basically meets the criteria.

I don't even mind throwing out my own trash, as long as I'm not waiting 15 minutes to be served.

I've observed that there are two kinds of people in the world: Some grasp the fast food concept, and some just don't.

I was in my favorite establishment just last week, with only about three minutes to get it and go, when I got behind the dreaded Discerning Customer—a woman of about 60 who had obviously never been in a burger joint in her life and was attempting to have a meaningful dialog with the register clerk.

The conversation went something like this: "Hello, young man. I'd like one of your cheeseburger deluxes. Tell your chef that I'd like it medium, but not too pink in the middle. Now, does that come with regular mayonnaise or light? Well, I need the light. Watching my waistline, don't you know. And are the tomatoes nice and ripe? I don't want them unless they're sweet and juicy. Oh, and do you have Romaine lettuce? I don't really like iceberg. And I'd like the bun grilled lightly..."

This went on for about five minutes, while the guy at the register stared blankly into space, trying to figure out which button to push, and customers stacked up behind the woman like they were waiting for Shania Twain tickets.

It's apparent to me that we ought to offer seminars to those people who have just recently discovered fast food. The trick is to talk fast and not offer too much information.

On a recent trip with a friend of mine, who's more of a twigs and berries kind of guy, he decided to throw caution to the wind and have a burger. We stopped at a Burger King, where, by the way, the food and service were both just fine.

Our plan was to sample the standard fare: a Whopper for him, two Juniors for me, and two fries—and that's how we should have ordered them: just that fast. However, being a rookie, my friend (we'll call him Tom) felt compelled to brief the register girl prior to ordering.

He leaned over to her, glanced around, lowered his voice to a near whisper (you'd have thought he was divulging the whereabouts of a buried treasure map), and said, "We're going to have three hamburgers: one Whopper, two Junior Whoppers, and two large fries."

We'll, that's what we got. The bill came to about 10 bucks, and *six* sandwiches appeared on our tray.

I tried to explain that she just punched them in as he ordered them. He countered by saying that he was just trying to be helpful and let her know our intentions ahead of time. I suggested that because everybody in the place was ordering pretty much the same thing, there was really no need to give her a heads-up. This only seemed to irritate him, and I finally decided that trying to explain fast-food protocol to a health-food jock is like trying to teach table etiquette to a bear.

The good news was that after three burgers, I didn't need supper.

Dorm Food

There's really nothing quite like the aroma of leftover Salisbury steaks simmering in their own lard to send your taste buds into a frenzy.

I know whereof I speak, for I had the good fortune to attend one of Michigan's state universities back in the '70s, and for two years I lived on that tantalizing dorm food. This was before the days of salad bars and counting fat grams. If you were hungry, you went back for seconds of instant potato flakes and gravy.

Hence, the term "freshman 16," which was the average college student weight gain during his/her first year on campus. Many a skinny little freshman was transformed into an overnight butterball through this process.

D-Rations weren't all bad, but they certainly were an experience. Let me tell you about some of our chef's specialties.

First on the list has to be Jell-O. It's cheap, it's colorful, it's versatile, and it requires little or no talent to prepare. It's even good—just not 17 days in a row.

Our staff used to make just enough to feed a small country, and on Day One they'd feed it to us plain. Fine. The next day they'd slide a lettuce leaf under it, and presto: It was salad. It was *still* salad on Day Three, but on Day Four they yanked the lettuce and plopped on a glob of whipped cream, and you had your basic dessert. Yummy.

Enough you say? I think not.

After several days in the dessert phase, the now-turning-green whipped cream was scraped off, and the Jell-O was carved up into those nifty little cubes that can be eaten by hand or used to patch tires.

Cole slaw was my next-favorite dish. Actually, I never tried eating it, but just the sight of it swimming in a quart of that milky dressing was enough to ruin anyone's appetite. We'd tolerate it for about six days in a row, and then finally get tired of looking at it every time we went through the line. Then everyone would take it, dump it out in a giant mound on one of the dinner tables, stick our forks in it, and leave. This at least forced them to throw the slimy stuff out, and it allowed us to register a silent protest. (This was the early '70s; protests were the thing back then.)

Have you tried the hard rolls? Our crack team of pastry specialists added new meaning to the term by baking the same rolls day after day, warming them over and over, until it took a chainsaw to crack the outer shell. They were like petrified dinosaur eggs. However, they made great hall hockey pucks. We'd shoot them at the RA's door, and a really good one that had been properly cured would last for 15 or 20 slapshots before exploding in shower of croutons.

Their other specialty was breakfast in general. The eggs were this weird off-white color and sort of rubbery, and they had a peculiar odor that I couldn't possibly describe, although my old junior high locker room came pretty close. I'm not convinced that they actually came from chickens.

The pancakes were amazing. Each one was the size of a dinner plate and a half-inch thick. You could pour an eight-ounce tumbler of syrup on a stack, bend over to pick up your napkin, and in the time it took you to sit back up, the syrup would be gone. Bone dry. No evidence that it had ever been there. These babies weren't exactly long on taste (unless you count aftertaste), but they made wonderful sponges. I'm surprised the Huggies people haven't tried to harness this secret for their diapers.

There were so many other delightful delicacies, but reminiscing about them is making me a little nauseated, and I'm concerned about latent psychological trauma, like a flashback to the days in 'Nam. Perhaps it's time to terminate this little trip down memory lane.

So, if you're off to college, heed these words of advice. Stick to cereal, salad, muffins, and anything else that doesn't require preparation. Avoid anything that ends in the word "casserole." Don't even think about trying the tuna boats. And, in general, if you don't recognize it, don't eat it.

Dinner Is Pointless

Every evening, when I get home from work and walk through the door, I sniff the air in anxious anticipation of what diet plan we might be on this week.

If I'm greeted by the delicious aroma of bacon sizzling in the pan, I know it's Atkins week. If I'm assaulted by the pungent smell of simmering cauliflower, it means we're counting points on Weight Watchers. If I don't smell anything, it must be my turn to cook.

You may find yourself frustrated and confused by all the latest diets. Let's say you're hosting a little dinner shindig at your house. Two of your guests are counting points, another is counting carbs, one is a vegetarian, and the fifth is eating nothing but cabbage soup.

What should you do?

No, really, I'm asking: What should you do? Close the drapes and turn off the lights?

It's easier to solve a quadratic equation than it is to solve the great diet dilemma. The only thing I've determined from all these diet crazes is that potatoes are *out*. They are high in carbs, high in points, and avoided by all. If the Irish Potato Famine had happened during modern times, nobody would have noticed.

The problem with living with people who are on various diet plans is that if <u>they're</u> not eating it, <u>you're</u> not eating it. Try walking in with some Chinese food or an 18-inch Carnivore's Deluxe Pizza, and you'll hear, "You're not going to eat that in front of me, are you?"

The other commonly heard quote is, "If it's not in the house, I won't be tempted to eat it." In English, this means that there are no cookies, potato chips, or gooey dark chocolate treats of any kind in the pantry, and you'd best not try to smuggle them in.

If I had to rate the diets I've been on by association, I'd have to say that the low-carb plans are the tastiest and most filling. Dinner is likely to be a ham sandwich—but not as we know it. A no-carb ham sandwich is a breadless wonder: three fried eggs, a layer of Swiss, a layer of sharp cheddar, four strips of bacon, Ranch dressing, and enough butter to lube your van, all engulfed by two slabs of ham the size of Frisbees.

The problem with the previously mentioned sandwich is that, if the person on the plan eats three of them a day, she'll be down 14 pounds in the first month. If I, on the other hand, try to be a team player and eat perhaps one a day, in two weeks I'll look like Chris Farley.

Therefore, what we need is a new diet plan messiah—the first recipient of the Pulitzer Prize for Purging Poundage. Atkins was a genius, but I'd miss bread and pasta too much. Perhaps there are foods which, if eaten individually, are bad for your health, but in combination are actually good for you. We just need someone to discover the magic formulas.

I'm waiting to find out that, although T-bone steaks and French fries aren't recommended for your heart, if combined with high doses of fresh raspberries, chocolate-almond ice cream, pecan rolls, and a pretentious little Chablis produced only in the south of France, they'll actually lower your cholesterol and flush excess fats from your system.

In the meantime, tonight it's either steak with a side of ham and eggs, or Brussels sprouts with a garnish of celery.

Please Pass the Rattlesnake

I must admit to having only cursory knowledge of what goes on at some of your higher echelon's fancy cocktail parties. Most of the social gatherings I attend involve jeans, T-shirts, and going Dutch treat on pizza and cold beverages.

However, I have it on good authority that the bigger the party, the more exotic the food. The tradeoff is that you may have to stand around in a three-piece suit listening to some big shots bragging about their yachts, stock portfolios, golf games, and plastic surgeries, but everything has its price.

These people expect the oldest Scotch, the finest champagne, and a smorgasbord of unique delicacies specially prepared to tantalize the palate.

This brings us to today's topic: Do you know what a delicacy really is?

Although some would view it as something rare or luxurious to eat, I'm afraid I must beg to differ. Loosely translated, it should be defined as, "Some sort of peculiar organic food substitute that someone once managed to swallow without chucking all over the other distinguished guests at a party."

Then (and this is the really fun part) in the spirit of the Emperor's New Clothes, none of the other lemmings wanted to admit to being the only one who thought it tasted like dead rodent, so of course they all raved about it.

In time, these nasty little offerings became the repast of choice at virtually all of your upper crust's major social gatherings, and the tradition continues ad infinitum, even building up steam as demented chefs dream up new ways to administer gastric torture. The fact that an ounce or two of most of these goodies will probably cost more than an average mortgage payment is hardly a deterrent. In fact, it only seems to add to the mystique.

So, you ask, how can you tell whether the snot-like substance you're putting on your cracker is actually edible or you'll want to deposit it in a nearby plant? It's considered poor etiquette to start hocking into your napkin while standing at the *hors d'oeuvres* table, so it's imperative not to place anything into your mouth that you don't actually intend to swallow.

Therefore, allow me to offer these few simple words of advice:

IF IT GOES BY AN ALIAS, DON'T EAT IT.

The reason you are offered caviar, calamari, and pâté is that nobody would be caught dead with a mouthful of processed salted sturgeon eggs, pieces and parts of prepared squid, or ground bile-secreting gland of goose. Get it? Don't be fooled by clever disguises or things that allegedly taste like chicken. A rose by any other name growing in a manure pile would smell...

Uh, well, you get the picture.

So, if you want to rub elbows with the in-crowd, my suggestion is to stick to the veggie plates, jumbo shrimp, and the salted cashews. Just say <u>no</u> to the raw oysters (there's a reason they have to slather them with hot sauce before slurping them down), and the same advice goes double for the Rocky Mountain variety. You're more than welcome to my share of the escargots.

As for the rattlesnake—well, it doesn't, so have the chicken wings, instead. Besides, they're only 89 cents a pound.

Birdseed: It's for the Birds

While sitting at my computer the other day, munching on a bag of Famous Amos chocolate chip cookies from one vending machine and washing it down with a bottle of Coke from another, I happened across the recommended dietary requirements for your average adult and the minimum number of daily servings. Sheeesh.

It seems that I (and you, too, unless you're below average) have been coming up a bit short on the intake scale. We're supposed to be chowing down five servings of whole grains, three vegetables, three fruits, two legumes—which include beans and (yuk) tofu—one helping of seeds or nuts, and some vitamin B12, found in eggs and dairy. We're talking every day. Whew. I may need to quit my job and take up grazing full-time.

Anyhow, I did the math, and that's 15 servings of healthy stuff. This doesn't include the Twinkies, potato chips, Snickers bars, ice cream, pop, burgers, fries, and all the other garbage that makes up 90 percent of our real diets. Fortunately, the article I read listed sweets as a food group (well, duh) and under number of servings, it said "optional." To me, that means "Consume until full."

My concern is how I'm going to meet the minimum requirements without ordering tofu takeout and having myself cloned. My daily routine consists of cereal and a banana for breakfast, and a light lunch of salad and soup (possibly in the legume category, if barley or minestrone). If I count the milk on the cereal as my B12 and redo the math on the old TI-30, the result is a bit daunting.

Starting at dinner time, I need to start packing in four whole grains, one serving of legumes, two vegetables, two fruits, and possibly some birdseed, not to mention the "optional" category. I'll have to move some furniture and set up an "All you can possibly eat" buffet in the dining room.

For those of you who share my concern, I'm thinking we need a creative solution. Otherwise, we're stuck with celery and wheat bread. Although I haven't confirmed this, I believe that some strawberry topping on your evening dish of ice cream may count as a fruit. Since peanuts count as a legume (I like that word), the aforementioned ice cream should be Rocky Road.

We're not done yet. Think pizza. It's nature's perfect food.

The crust is made from grains (I think). Just take two generous slices piled high with peppers, onions, and tomato sauce, and you've got a big chunk of the veggies, fruits, and grains covered. I checked. The tomato is actually a fruit.

About the only thing remaining is that last pesky double serving of whole grains. Well, the news is still good. That pizza is going to be pretty tough to swallow without a nice, cold beverage (or in this case, two). I just looked it up. Beer is produced by the brewing and fermentation of starches derived from (drum roll, please) cereal grains, most notably malted barley or wheat. That means that, in addition to its whole-grain goodness, it might even double as a legume.

For those of you who prefer not to imbibe, the above is only a guideline. You can skip the beer, drink iced tea, and go with four slices of pizza. The birdseed is your problem. I was just happy to discover that I've been on the right track all along.

Musings of a Cereal Killer

If you read the title, you know that I'm a diabolical (and I like that word) cereal killer.

I can go through a box of Total Raisin Bran in three days, four at the outside. Sure, scrambled eggs and bacon and English muffins are tasty, but my morning mainstay is cereal and milk.

Now it's time for true confessions. Although I like Wheaties and Grape Nuts and other fibrous, nutritious repasts (try that five times fast), my real passion is pre-sweetened *anything*. Yes, I'm talking Alpha Bits and Cocoa Krispies and even Trix. I don't care if they're for kids. Frost it and glaze it and fill it with empty calories—and I'll have a double helping.

If you bump into me at the grocery store and notice a box of Cocoa Puffs in my cart, you might logically assume that it's for my grandchildren. OK, we'll go with that. I suppose they can have a bowl—if there's any left.

Meanwhile, I need to raise an issue.

When I was growing up, we ate Sugar Pops and Sugar Smacks and Sugar Crisp. Note the common theme. Then, sometime in the early 1990s, that all changed. Apparently, some former cult followers of Euell Gibbons, or perhaps some overly zealous soccer moms, or maybe it was (were?) the Communists convinced the general public that sugar was bad. After that, everything went by an alias.

Take a walk down the cereal aisle. You'll see Corn Pops and Honey Smacks and Super Golden Crisp. Honey Smacks, my ear; it's the same stuff we were eating in 1980. You can put an Obama bumper sticker on Rush Limbaugh's Mercedes, but that doesn't make him a Democrat.

My reason for bringing this up is that it may be time for the Battle Creek brain trust to rethink their strategy and reinstitute their old brand names. Have you noticed what college kids are consuming these days? It's <u>not</u> brown rice and organic vegetables. I saw a student the other day with a big slab of pepperoni pizza, a bag of chips, a king-size Snickers bar, and a Monster energy drink.

I'm suggesting that, instead of trying to camouflage their products, the cereal companies may want to embrace the Facebook generation and take a page from Jolt Cola, which hyped itself as having "all the sugar and twice the caffeine." If you tell any frat rat that there's a cereal out there that will make his brain spin and help him survive an all-nighter, he'll be all over it like wet on water.

I'm working on the ad campaign now. No Yolks noodles claim, "We don't have what you don't need." Boring. How about, "Sugar Stars: Sure, they're bad for you, but they'll give you a buzz." I bet they won't be able to keep them on the shelves.

In our next episode, we'll examine the virtues of Cheez Whiz.

Gas Station Cuisine

As I've gotten older, I've noticed that my palate has changed, and I enjoy foods that I didn't care for at a younger age. I prefer dry wine to sweet, dark chocolate over milk, and I've even developed a taste for beets. No, really.

In my twenties, I'd have been happy with canned soup and boring old pot roast. However, it seems that my taste buds have become more sophisticated. (They have, even though I haven't.) Now I rather crave beef bourguignon and tomato bisque and baklava and some other B-word foods that nobody can spell or pronounce.

However, lest you think I'm getting all snooty and hoity-toity, I have a confession to make (drum roll, please): I love gas station pizza. I mean I absolutely <u>crave</u> gas station pizza.

There, I said it. Wow, I feel so liberated.

I don't know what it is, but something about the smell of pizza by the slice or fried chicken mixed with the sweet aroma of gasoline fumes just sends my taste buds into a frickin' finger-lickin' frenzy. (Try *that* five times fast.)

I think I need to begin a new career as the Midwest counterpart of those New York restaurant critics. You know, the kind who grace some establishment with their presence, consume $400 worth of exotic food and wine on someone else's dime, and then have the temerity (I just got a new thesaurus) to write something snotty in *The New Yorker*.

Of course, I'll need a cool new food critic handle/alias. How about Epicurious George? That has a nice ring to it.

Anyhow, I picture myself cruising through rural Michigan in search of the perfect gas station or convenience store cuisine. Presentation will be important. If it's tanning itself in the warming oven, equidistant between the 5-Hour Energy display and the cash register, well, that's as good as it gets.

I already know of several great haunts. If you're riding your bike on the rail trail through Hersey and find you're feeling a bit peckish (I like that word), there's a gas station there that will sell you a square, half-acre slice of pizza that is absolutely life-changing. The fact that you can snarf it down at a picnic table within 20 feet of the gas pumps only adds to its appeal.

There's a little store in Rogers Heights where a very nice woman with pretty cool body art will sell you a complete dinner with chicken tenders that almost melt in your mouth. And if you're on a road trip, there's a station in Lake Isabella that my wife says has the best pizza on the planet. When I lived in Houghton in the '70s, I knew someone who drove 100 miles to Marquette just to go to McDonald's. That seemed excessive, but I'd drive 30 miles for this pizza.

There's also a station in Hesperia that not only has pizza, but also specializes in "fry it and buy it" cuisine. So, after slogging around the White River in search of the elusive salmon, you can treat yourself to fish or chicken or French fries or hush puppies or anything else that greases your fancy. Just pick your poison.

So, I'm off to start my new career. If you see someone licking his fingers and taking notes in some out-of-the-way establishment, it's probably me. Be sure to say hi. Remember to call me George.

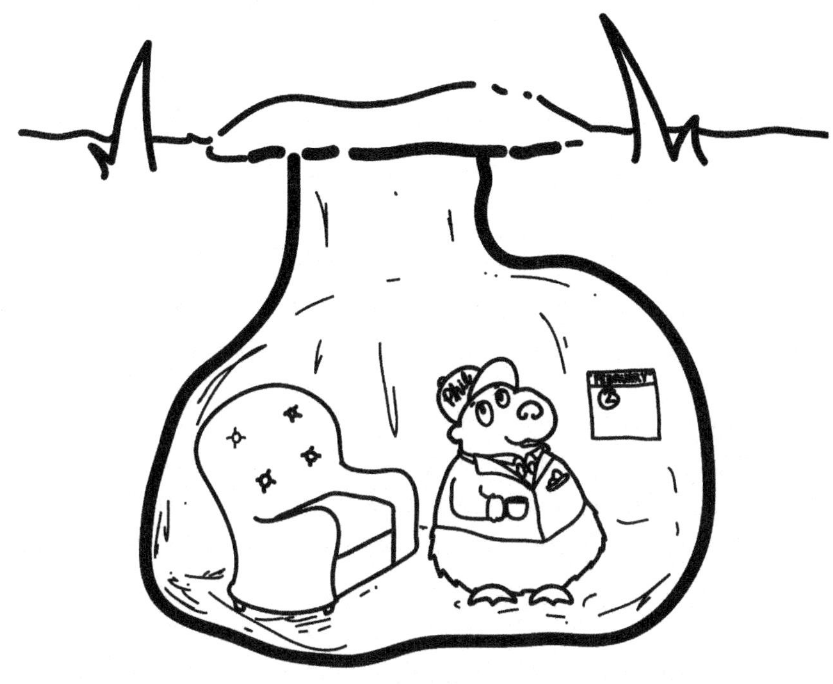

Chapter 2

Holidays

Ah, the holidays, a time for family, food and festivities. They're also the perfect opportunity to regain the 10 pounds you just spent six months sweating off at the gym, to visit some old relatives you've never really liked, and to run up a small mountain of debt on your credit cards.

Local Man Malled By Christmas Shoppers

Well, the holiday season is nearly upon us, and with it comes the dreaded obligatory trip to the mall.

In my opinion, the nicest Christmas gift you can give your spouse or significant other is to not invite them to join you on a shopping trip. Men and women spending that much quality time together is a recipe for disaster.

As it turns out, some women actually enjoy shopping (no, really). They will call in sick or even take vacation days from work so they can spend all day pawing through acres of endless deals. In Minnesota, they have the Queen Mother of all malls, and they'll spend hundreds of dollars to fly there for a whole weekend, just so they can save an additional 10 percent at Eddie Bauer.

Men are entirely different. They are not there to enjoy the ambience nor to savor the moment. Twenty minutes into the shopping experience we're looking at our watches.

I remember my last trip as though it was yesterday. I was going to the Really Big Super Duper New Mall in the Grand Rapids area during the peak of the Christmas shopping season. I found a convenient parking place in section XX99, somewhere on the outskirts of Zeeland. Luckily, I'd packed enough provisions to get me through the long hike to the mall entrance, but I inadvertently ate one too many sandwiches and ran out of breadcrumbs to drop before I reached HH25. Oh, well.

I shinnied up a light pole, discovered that I could actually see my destination in the hazy distance, and proceeded with my journey. I'd worry about finding my car later. (Maybe I'd buy a GPS unit inside.)

I entered through one of the major department stores, carefully noting my path (left at men's shoes, right at outerwear, left again at women's undergarments, right at the blonde clerk wearing more cologne that Sam Malone), and finally I was there.

The scene that confronted me could only be described as utter chaos. There were people everywhere.

I stepped out into the open, then jumped back immediately as some woman with a shrill voice and a spandex suit yelled, "Track!" Eight people in similar garb huffed passed me, legs churning and arms pumping, a look of disdain on their faces as they sneered at me.

I'd heard about mall walkers, but I didn't realize they traveled in packs. Further inspection revealed moms pushing toddlers in strollers, teen hoods with hundred dollar shoes and their pants around their knees, pale businessmen in gray suits, and so many others that it looked like the U.N.

My original plan (novice that I was) had been to simply walk in and proceed directly to the sports store to buy my brother a new fishing reel. Obviously, it would take more strategy. I decided to zig and zag, dashing from safe zone to safe zone until I reached my final destination.

My first stop was a small island with a vender hawking cell phones. I paused, caught my breath, and headed for the information desk, pausing only briefly as I passed the all-red Victoria's Secret. (Now I know where anorexic hookers get their stuff.)

From there, I was on to that little living room with the Naugahyde couches located in the middle of the mall, where men of all ages were sitting, sequestered, looking at their watches. One poor slob said he'd been there since Tuesday. I had a brief moment of melancholy as I wondered how many Naugas had given their all just so these guys could sit around in comfort waiting for their wives, but this was no time to be sentimental. I could see the entrance to my store, and I sprinted for pay dirt.

The scene was something out of Orwell. There were 12 people clutching and grabbing at a sale rack of sport shirts, snarling and cursing at each other and drowning out a cheery rendition of "Deck the Halls" being piped in through the mall-com. Two other guys were practicing their WWF moves as they grappled for a pair of hunting boots.

Now I understood. This was a blood sport.

I headed for the fishing section, sliding in undetected and snatching the last Garcia reel out from under the gaze of another customer who was just a little slow on the draw. Too bad, pal. His tirade was a distant whine as I headed for the register and certain victory.

I waited in line for 20 minutes while some woman tried to get the register clerk to decide whether the blue or burgundy jogging suit looked best, and finally...

I made it!

I reached for my wallet, which had all my cash and credit cards, and only then remembered that I'd left it on the front seat when I got lunch at the McDonald's drive-thru.

Defeated, I left the reel on the counter and trudged back through the mall, trying to remember whether my car was in XX or ZZ. No matter. The wallet was safely locked in the car—with my keys.

Christmas Giving: It's a Phase

Uh-oh. What happened? I just woke up and found out it's already December.

I had all these grandiose plans of making my list and checking it twice and being done shopping before everyone stopped being nice, but now it appears that I'm going to be joining the rush with all the other crazoids.

Actually, it's not entirely my fault. Our family did the whole Thanksgiving thing twice, with enough leftovers to feed Montana for a week. As a result, I've spent the past several days eating turkey sandwiches, turkey casseroles, turkey soup, sweet and sour turkey, turkey Jell-O, turkey fudge, etc. In short, I've had so much tryptophan that I've been wandering around in a foggy haze for the past couple weeks, so it's not surprising that I lost track of time.

Anyhow, with the leftovers finally finished and some industrial-strength caffeine in my system, I'm ready to head for the mall. Unfortunately, I'm afraid one trip to that dreaded psycho ward may put a damper on the whole season. There's heavy traffic, remote parking, long lines, pushing and shoving, and that's just filling up at the gas station on the way down.

Couldn't we simplify the whole thing, even for one year?

In the old days (I was watching an old episode of "Little House"), Santa would put something in Laura's stocking, like maybe a new penny, some peppermint candy, and a pair of hand-knit mittens, and she was thrilled.

These days, it seems like St. Nick has been replaced by Art Van. Plus, as our families age, it gets tougher and tougher to buy something that someone really wants or needs.

With the exception of my daughters, who are wonderful at making or finding sentimental gifts, it seems like gift-giving gradually degenerates through a number of phases.

In Phase 1, the kids are small, and they're excited about everything they get, like dolls and sleds and plastic army soldiers. In return, they give their parents something they made in school, like a plaster handprint or a picture frame. I (sniff) love this phase.

In Phase 2, we all have everything we need, and our extended families have way too many people to buy expensive gifts for everyone. So, we have Christmas as usual with our immediate families, and we draw names with a dollar limit for the rest of the relatives. This isn't so bad, as the gifts are still a surprise, but we've cut back on the shopping volume a bit.

In Phase 3, we've discovered that most of these gifts don't fit, aren't needed (like a pneumatic golf ball washer), or are ugly. So, we tell them exactly what we want, like a crockpot, and they "surprise" us with it on Christmas Day.

In Phase 4, we go out and buy the crockpot that we want, and then have a third party secretly deliver it to the family member who drew our name, so she can "surprise" us with it on Christmas Day.

In Phase 5, it's getting more difficult for some people to get out and shop, so they just give us a token gift, like a sleeve of golf balls, and with it a $50 bill and instructions to go out and buy the crockpot we want.

I can see Phase 6 coming, where we simply exchange $50 bills.

Phase 7 is the one that scares me, because it's when we've decided to just forget the whole thing and stay home with the money already in our wallets. My only hope is that, as our kids have children, we return to Phase 1.

The Tryptophan Express

I've always loved Thanksgiving.

As a kid, it meant going to Grandpa and Grandma's house, seeing my cousins, smelling the wonderful aromas of all the great food, and basically just having one of the best days of the year.

Thanksgiving should be a time to give thanks for all our blessings, to perhaps enjoy the company of family and those closest to us, and to chow down on some of the traditional foods the Pilgrims feasted on, like *tofurkey*. But after asking around, I realized that not everyone seems to share my romantic notion of the holidays.

In a little more cynical vein, here's what I heard: One person in every household—be it a mom, aunt, or grandma, but definitely the alpha female—is basically in charge of everything. She starts preparing early, sometime around the Fourth of July, to make all the pies and candies and cookies and snacks that will be inhaled on Thanksgiving Day.

Then, on that fateful morning, she rolls out of the sack at about 3 a.m., rinses a bird the size of an ostrich, prepares the stuffing, pares half a bushel of potatoes, builds a relish tray, sets the table, and, well, you get the picture. By 7 a.m. she's ready for a shot of Bourbon.

Then there are the traveling guests. They have to be out of bed by about 6 a.m. so everyone can shower, eat breakfast (not too much—you'll spoil your dinner), and be on the road by 7:30.

Teenagers especially love this part. Not only do they get to rise and shine on the military clock, but they get to spend three hours each way sharing quality time with their parents and kid brother in the minivan.

The whole gaggle arrives at Aunt Alpha's house by 11 a.m. and, while snacking on the previously mentioned goodies, proceeds to engage in *traditional Thanksgiving activities.*

For the teens, this means finding a closet somewhere and calling their sequestered counterparts on their cell phones. For the women, it's not only a time to begin final meal preparations, but also a social time to catch up on all the important family stuff they've missed since the last holiday season.

For the men—<u>all</u> the men—it means FOOTBALL.

They'll rush to the living room, plant themselves in every available chair surrounding the television set, and, with absolutely no conversation nor acknowledgement of their fellow beings, begin watching the pre-game show about the Lions and whoever drew the long straw to clobber them this week.

Dinnertime arrives, and Alpha and the other women, in a beautifully coordinated effort, manage to get all the food to the buffet table at the perfect serving temperature.

They then call the other family members, several of whom are still hiding in closets, and the rest who can't come just yet because the Lions are threatening to score.

Finally, as the potatoes stiffen and the gravy congeals, everyone straggles into the dining room. After a word of Grace, the devouring begins.

Thanksgiving is a time for eating foods we rarely see during the rest of the year. Besides the turkey, there are mashed potatoes, dressing, cranberry sauce, pearl onions, sweet potatoes, squash, oysters, cheesy cauliflower, green beans with French-fried onions, and stuff like that.

Here's where the tension starts.

As it turns out, the younger children don't necessarily like everything. Specifically, they don't care for the potatoes, dressing, cranberries, onions, sweet potatoes, squash, oysters, cauliflower, green beans and stuff. They're having turkey and SpaghettiOs.

Three other members of the group are counting points, so the potatoes and dressing are definitely out. Two more are on Atkins, so none for them, either. That means Alpha has boiled 57 potatoes for six people.

Finally, after the three kinds of pie are finished, the women start clearing the table and psyching up to tackle the disaster area known as the kitchen.

The men, recognizing the heroic efforts made by their counterparts, attempt to ease their burden by bolting back the living room for the second half. There, with 8,000 calories each and a heavy dose of tryptophan flowing through their bloodstreams, they'll fall asleep—all of them, until it's time to go home. The only saving grace is that they'll be spared the final agonizing quarter of Detroit's 45-3 loss to the second-worst team in the NFL.

Finally, at about 5 p.m., with a rumble in their bellies and an aching in their hearts, they all pile back in the minivan and head for home.

Happy Thanksgiving, everyone!

All About Leftovers

Every year we have about 50 pounds of leftovers after the Thanksgiving holiday.

This should not come as a surprise. We have eight people at the table and enough food to feed a garrison. First, the guests spend an hour eating a variety of *hors de,* uh, appetizers, like sausage-stuffed mushrooms and cheese dip with bread and crackers, so they are already full. There's no way they're going to finish 16 mashed potatoes and two bags of bread stuffing.

Luckily, we have a wonderful set of those plastic storage containers, and they stack beautifully, so we absolutely fill the refrigerator with turkey, dressing, mashed potatoes, gravy, green beans, squash, and everything else we couldn't finish. It's enough food for a week.

That's where the theory starts to break down. For the next five days you're feeling not only bloated, but also a bit guilty about all the fat grams and calories you snarfed down on Thursday, so you eat cereal and tomato soup and salad.

Then, you're no longer in the mood for leftovers. The term "left" is associated with liberal, and the word "over," although it has several connotations, can refer to no longer having an interest in something. Well, that about sums it up for me: We have a *liberal* stack of aging food in the refrigerator, and my interest in it is *over*.

Again, it's a timing issue. Even if you would consider reheating them, the leftovers have been seasoning for over a week. The potatoes have reached the consistency of hardened clay. The gravy is starting to look like Jell-O, and the Jell-O looks like gravy. Any leftover salad is in full wilt mode, and the stuffing is as soggy (not to mention as appetizing) as wet gym socks.

This should be your cue to pull out everything except the sliced turkey and run it immediately down the garbage disposal, but, of course, you can't, because they're too good to throw away, and some starving child in some third-world country would be thrilled with them, and boy, this sentence is really running on.

So, you put them all back, neatly stacked, and they continue to season for another three weeks, again completely ignored. This is not good.

After that amount of time, you won't actually be able to distinguish the mashed potatoes from the corn casserole, as they'll both have the same consistency and greenish hue. They may also become aware of their surroundings, start growing tentacles, and try to escape.

At some point, you'll be afraid to open the refrigerator door, and will have to begin eating all your meals out. By the time you actually make the decision to get rid of them, your leftovers will have fused to their Tupperware containers, and you'll have to throw out the whole kit and caboodle (I love that phrase), plastic and all.

Don't let this happen to you. If you're having 10 people for dinner, cook just enough for eight. Save the turkey, and get rid of the rest of the insidious residuals without ever letting them find a new home in your refrigerator.

I'm just trying to help.

New Year's Revelation

It's only days away, and the coming of the new year always seems to drag along with it a perceived obligation on our parts to improve our lives in some way.

So, with a new resolve, we (again) promise ourselves to lose 20 pounds, or to start writing that novel, or to learn a foreign language, or to stop smoking, or whatever.

Unfortunately, all these grandiose plans seem to have about the same lifespan as a mayfly, and our inability to follow through leaves us feeling even more aware of our own shortcomings.

Therefore, this year, unlike other years, I have made an entire list of New Year's resolutions that I believe I can keep. These include:

1. I'm not going to purchase anything or donate to any cause over the phone.
2. Related to No. 1 above, I will no longer be more than briefly polite to any telemarketer. If they persist after, "Thanks, I'm not interested," it's open season.
3. I will not watch or listen to the same commercial more than twice in the same day. Likewise, I will immediately change the channel whenever some motor-mouthed caffeine junky reads the same 800-number to me four times in 10 seconds.
4. I won't go on any fad diets.
5. I won't listen to any rap "music."
6. I will find more time for trout fishing.
7. I will not open nor respond to unsolicited emails.
8. I will not fill out nor participate in any surveys.
9. I will not agree to serve on any committee that doesn't interest me, even if it is the politically correct thing to do.

10. I will eat no squash, liver, sweet potatoes, okra, or squid. (I tried using this for Lent, as well, but my wife said it really wasn't in the spirit of the season.)

11. I will watch no reruns of "Gilligan's Island," "The Brady Bunch," or "The Munsters."

12. I will not watch any "reality" television shows or soap operas.

13. I won't stand in line for more than three minutes in any fast-food restaurant.

14. I won't get any tattoos nor have any parts of my body pierced.

15. I will not dye nor gel my hair.

This was so easy that I decided to start at Thanksgiving. So far, I'm batting 1.000, and I feel great about myself. It's all just a matter of setting realistic goals.

Best of luck with yours.

Happy Woodchuck Day

Yes, folks, it's that time of year again. We are mere hours away from that holiday of holidays, the most eagerly anticipated and celebrated event of the year: Groundhog Day.

Wow, what a great scam. The people of Punxsutawney, Pennsylvania, have somehow managed to take an oversized muskrat, elevated him to rock-star status, and created an event that brings their little town fame, riches, and national recognition.

Frankly, cities all over the country wish they'd thought of it first.

In case you just arrived here from Mars or someplace, the legend of Groundhog Day has Scottish roots. It's based on an old couplet (I learned a new word today) that goes, "If Candlemas Day is bright and clear, there'll be two winters in the year."

Anyhow, every February 2nd, a large rodent named Punxsutawney Phil is dragged out of his heated condo up on Gobbler's Knob (shouldn't they use a turkey?), and if he sees his shadow, we'll spend the next six weeks cranking up the old Toro.

Maybe I'm just jealous, but I think it's time we shed a little light on this blessed event. First off, there's nothing particularly special about Phil. He's a bit overweight and only about a "3" on the Handsome Meter.

He's also not much of a performer.

Heck, my dog can sit up and do high fives, and Phil's not even in his league. I have no idea how a short, average-looking creature lacking any measurable talent can achieve national stardom, but I guess if it works for Regis, it can work for Phil.

Part of my negative attitude comes from the fact that Phil has gotten a little big for his fuzzy, little britches. He's not just some poor woodchuck foraging in the woods and huddling in his hole to avoid the winter chill. He actually has a custom-made, electrically heated den.

Also, I can't confirm it, but I've heard from a reliable source that he has an agent. From what I can gather, during the off-season he is pampered beyond his (or my) wildest dreams. He's always flying to exotic locations, staying at Holiday Inns, lavished with expensive gifts, and eating the finest vegetarian cuisine created by French chefs.

If that's not bad enough, I hear he has a number of understudies. At the risk of bursting your bubble, it's entirely possible that, when the furry little forecaster emerges from his den on the morning of the 2nd, what you're seeing could just as easily be Bill or Will, or perhaps even Lil!

Meanwhile, the real deal is sipping tall umbrella drinks on the French Riviera. It's really quite disappointing. Plus, about 90 percent of the time, the little runt sees his shadow, and we have to put up with snow until Memorial Day.

Well of *course* he sees his shadow. He's a hibernating animal. All he has to do is stroll out, say, "Yep, there it is," and he can crawl back down and take a nap for six more weeks, with plenty of tasty drinks and nobody bothering him.

Well, maybe it's time to stop whining and be a little proactive.

First of all, we should move the whole thing, lock, stock, and burrow, to Michigan. The likelihood of the sun popping out around here in February is about the same as Ralph Nader winning a presidential election.

So, if you want an early end to winter, put old Phil on the next bus to Big Rapids, because his shadow will be nothing but a distant memory. If that doesn't work, maybe we should start our own stupid animal event. All we need is a possum or a red fox that's willing to give up his freedom in return for being treated like British royalty.

Meanwhile, there's no big rush on tuning up the lawn mower.

Happy Fertility Day

Well, guys, it's that time again.

Here comes that holiday/observance when, if you buy her a new toaster, you're a complete jerk, and if you buy her candy, you're insensitive, because you should *know* she's on a diet, and if you don't buy her candy, are you insinuating that she doesn't really need it.

It's very perplexing.

As it turns out, our modern St. Valentine's Day originated as the Roman festival of Lupercalia, which was a fertility celebration held on February 15th. First, the names of girls were written on paper and placed in jars, and men drew the names to see who their escorts would be for the festival. It was like a giant blind date lottery.

Then, goats were sacrificed, and the foreheads of two boys were marked with blood. The boys ran through the streets lashing people with fresh, slimy goat skin strips, and this supposedly helped increase fertility.

Party on, Garth.

Anyhow, the goat strips have long since gone by the wayside, along with fertility ceremonies in general. In fact, most parents of teenage girls in this country would be relieved if someone could concoct (I like that word) a way to *decrease* their fertility. Even for those interested in starting a family, there's no need to butcher a goat, because we now have tequila.

The most famous St. Valentine was a bishop who held double secret marriage ceremonies. At that time, Claudius became emperor and immediately decreed that soldiers couldn't be married. Apparently, the morale of his troops wasn't his first priority.

Anyhow, he figured that having spouses would distract them and make them weak. So, Valentine ignored the order and had a secret place where young soldiers could go to marry their lovers. This may have originated the idea of "Don't ask, don't tell."

Like most secrets, it didn't last long, and Valentine soon found himself wandering around without a head. In fact, and this is the scary part, there were actually *three* Christian saints by the name of Valentine—a priest in Rome, a bishop in Terni, and a third who was kicking around Africa. According to history (drum roll, please), they all died on February 14th!

Do you Google? Not sure? Well, plug in "people named Valentine," and the only two who come up are Karen the actor and Bobby the baseball manager.

Where are all the rest, you ask? I'm thinking they're being systematically, uh, removed on February 14th every year. This might explain Rudolf's changing his name to Valentino. I checked. He died in August.

I don't want to be a wet blanket, but if someone shuffles up to you on the street and says, "Hi, Valentine," I'm afraid you might find yourself doing a Luca Brasi impersonation and sleeping with the fishes.

So, please don't send me a card asking to "Be my Valentine." Instead, send me a big box of chocolates and ask me to be your goat-skin-lashing fertility festival escort.

Mad as a March Easter Bunny

Spring is a busy time for holidays, with Saint Patrick's Day signaling the melting of the snow and a return to brighter, sunnier days.

Many of you recently celebrated the patron saint of Ireland in traditional fashion, by wearing green plastic derbies, buttons that say, "Kiss Me, I'm almost 10% Irish!"

and playing Beer Pong until you had green foam coming from your nose.

Likewise, we have some peculiar practices at Easter. For a time, it seems that everyone takes leave of their senses. How else can you explain giving a live baby chick to someone as a gift? (FYI: Those cute little critters turn into real chickens, and they make lousy house pets.)

Some of you might wonder how a Christian holiday somehow morphed into a story about decorated eggs delivered by a rabbit. Well, folks, the early church leaders were pretty savvy. A large number of their parishioners still liked to practice pagan rites and traditions (like Beer Pong).

If the church had tried to get tough and ban these old habits, there would have been a lot of empty pews and nothing but dust in the collection plates. So, under the category of, "If you can't beat 'em, join 'em," the early church simply absorbed a number of pagan practices.

In the second century in Europe, the pagan spring festival was a rowdy Saxon fertility celebration (likely the predecessor of your current fraternity toga party) in honor of the Saxon Goddess Eastre (Ostara), whose sacred animal was a hare. The phrase "Mad as a March Hare" would certainly seem to accurately depict the mindset of both the rabbit and the male college student as winter turns to spring and their thoughts turn to romance. Anyhow, that's how we got the rabbit.

The eggs have long been a symbol of fertility and rebirth. Going back several hundred years, German children awaited the arrival of Oschter Haws (*Osterhase*), a cwazy wabbit who left colored eggs in nests for good children to discover on Easter morning.

So, behave yourself and eat your vegetables, because Mr. Haws and Mr. Claus are watching you!

Moving forward to present day, I have one bit of advice: If you plan to decorate and tuck away real hard-boiled eggs for your children to find, make sure you take inventory before you hide them. Otherwise—and I speak from experience—a day will come in July, probably a very warm and humid day at that, when you'll be quite sure that either the sewer just backed up or a large rodent cashed in his chips behind the wall. Further investigation will lead you to an oval-shaped, green, fuzzy thing that's been ripening behind the piano since early April.

Finally, if you plan to take part in an Easter egg hunt, remember that it's for the little ones. One of my fondest memories is of taking our kids down to the local park, where there was a sponsored hunt for Easter treats. Everyone had to stay behind the line until the official start, and then off went all the kids in search of chocolate candies and surprises.

Unfortunately, a number of their mothers didn't get the memo that the event was for children only, and they dived in to make sure that their little darlings got their fair share.

The resulting pandemonium looked like a 90 percent off sale at Abercrombie & Fitch, with gouging and kicking and elbows flying and a bunch of scared little kids trying to stay out of the way. It was *not* pretty.

My wife decided that I should intervene, and she suggested that I yell, "All you mothers get off the field!" However, I was concerned that it might be misinterpreted, and besides, several of them were bigger than I.

So, a very happy Easter to all of you.

Go easy on the sugar, and try to remember the real reason for the season. If you feel compelled to give someone a live animal, consider rescuing a dog or cat from your local animal shelter, and save the chicken for Sunday dinner.

Chapter 3

Sports and Outdoors

There's nothing like the smell of a junior high locker room or the agony of a three-hour budget meeting to make you yearn for hiking, biking, fishing, skiing, and anything involving fresh air, mosquitoes, and the great outdoors.

Lard-O-Mania

I was always envious of the basketball players at my high school. What a life!

They were involved in a sport that was actually fun to play, could eat anything they wanted, had at least one cheerleader on each arm at all times, and were the biggest of the BMOCs on campus.

I was in that *other* sport: wrestling.

We worked out constantly, wore heavy rubberized sweats, starved ourselves, and generally felt like crap all the time. Why? Just so we could make weight and wrestle some other poor slobs who weren't good enough to make their basketball teams, either.

Even though we didn't get the fan support and recognition that some other sports got, I was always proud that I went through it, because it required a total commitment of mind and body, and just getting through it was an accomplishment, and, boy, this sentence is sure running on.

That's why, as an ex-wrestler, an ex-real-wrestler, I really have to take exception with that televised nitro-garbage-mania that's piped into your living room on several channels almost every day of the week. You know, the show where two very large, long-haired, steroid-popping, tattooed beefcakes wearing micro-shorts play full-contact Twister, while some Howard Cosell wannabe tries to make us all believe that it really is a sporting event.

Hey, gang, let's check our Reality Quotients: How many of you have actually watched more than one of these wrestling matches on television? How many hope to one day be there in person? How many of you actually think it's real?

If you've raised your hand to any of these questions, you may be a candidate for therapy. Seriously, though, who are those people who actually go to these events and yell and scream for their heroes? I don't get it. Does someone pay them?

They can't really believe that Biff 1 is hitting Biff 2 in the face 16 times. (Wouldn't there be *some* swelling?) Or how about when Biff 3, spying Biff 4 lying on his back on the mat, does his drop move and drives his forearm into Biff 4's jaw?

These aren't Rocky movies. If you really smash a guy in the face, he's going to bleed, spit a few teeth, die, stuff like that.

Then, my personal favorite: Biff 5, having just been slammed to the canvas after taking several uppercuts to the chin, is now wandering around the ring with a groggy, semi-dazed look in his eye (not to be confused with the way he usually looks).

Biff 6, noticing that his opponent is feeling a bit under the weather, takes this opportunity to catapult himself back and forth across the ring, presumably to build up speed. As he hurtles by on his sixth pass, 350 pounds of prime beef traveling at the speed of a small sports car, Biff 5 rallies, regains his senses, sticks out his forearm, and clotheslines Biff 6. Bad Biff 5. Poor Biff 6.

Poor us, for sitting through this hogwash when we could have been watching "Brady Bunch" reruns.

To all of you who think this is what wrestling is really about, I urge you to attend your next high school meet.

However, you might be disappointed. There are no tag teams, no rhinos in skimpy trunks, and no punching in the face. All you'll see are a bunch of skinny, tired, over-trained, real athletes who wish they'd learned how to play hoops.

Olympic Mole Trapping

A number of you have written to me expressing concern that you once again didn't see my name on the USA roster at the most recent Olympic Games.

It's true; I wasn't there.

I suppose with all the events, I should have been able to medal in something, but I just couldn't find the right fit. The decision to withdraw my name from consideration was difficult and was not made frivolously. I considered the following events:

- **Beach Volleyball:** It's true that at 5-foot-11 and with a vertical leap of nearly eight inches, I could have been an impact player. Unfortunately, I don't look all that terrific in a thong bikini, and I was a bit concerned about traumatizing the viewing public.

- **Marathon**: My fault; I forgot to train until mid-July and simply didn't have the time to get down to 104 pounds and 1.2 percent body fat.
- **Individual Medley**: I considered the 400 meter I.M., but every time I try the Butterfly, I manage two strokes and sink to the bottom.
- **Gymnastics**: Last I checked (which was in 1968), I could still do a cartwheel and a round-off.
- **Synchronized Diving**: This could have been my best event, but I don't have a partner.
- **Basketball**: Aside from a complete lack of talent, I was afraid that, without a four-year, $60 million contract and 26 tattoos, I just wouldn't fit in with the rest of the guys.

You can see my dilemma. Actually, the only thing preventing me from participating in the Olympics was that my specialty areas haven't been made a part of the Games—yet. Here's my wish list for new events:

- **Olympic Mole Trapping**: I finally discovered the secret and have bagged six of the little lawn monsters. I believe they're trying to build a basement under my driveway. My neighbor Matt is up to 11 and is sure to win gold, but I'm an outside shot for medal contention.
- **Olympic Taxiing**: I once took two daughters and their three friends to six different events (choir, track

practice, gymnastics, babysitting, etc.) in five different locations in approximately 68 minutes, on time and without written instructions or a GPS.

- **Olympic Golfing**: I'm capable of consistently shooting in the low 60s. They play nine holes, right?
- **Olympic Furniture Hauling**: I just schlepped two daughters to Kansas City in four weeks, with an overstuffed pickup dragging two U-Haul trailers, packed to the gills, in the rain, around the big pond, dodging Chicago rush-hour traffic, without noticeably ruining a single piece of furniture.
- **Olympic Party Grilling**: On a good day, I can manage kebabs, burgers, Brats, ribs, and corn on the cob for 12—without excessive carbon buildup—and still keep one hand free for a cold beverage.

So, it's time to stop procrastinating and start training.

Marlin Perkins Meets the Crocodile Hunter

Long before the Crocodile Hunter and the plethora (I like that word) of other "Let's irritate a large reptile for no particular reason" shows, we had "Mutual of Omaha's Wild Kingdom." It featured Marlin Perkins, the aging, distinguished-looking star of the show, and Jim, his expendable sidekick.

As I recall, Jim didn't have a last name, much like Tonto. If you recall the basic storyline of every Lone Ranger episode, poor Tonto was always being sent to town to get the tar beat out of him by eight or 10 bad guys, or sent into the quicksand to see how deep it was, or perhaps used to sight in the Lone Ranger's pistol. This was perfectly understandable. The Lone Ranger rode around the Wild West in a crisp, powder-blue suit and white hat, and there wasn't a dry cleaner within 1,500 miles.

Well, Jim was very much in the same boat—er, canoe—without a paddle.

Every episode had essentially the same plot. In one, Marlin sent old Jim into a green, slimy swamp in chest-deep water to extract a large boa constrictor from its lair. This, of course, irritated the snake, which reacted by doing what boa constrictors always do.

Anyhow, the camera kept panning back and forth between Marlin, who was standing on the bank pointing and barking out unsolicited advice, and Jim, who had 18 feet of snake coiled around him and only his nose and right ear sticking out of the water.

This is where we got our "Marlin-isms." In his rather distinctive, whiney lisp, he'd say, "I stood on the bank while Jim grappled with the large serpent. Watch out for those teeth, Jim." Or, "I stayed in the truck while Jim grappled (he liked that word) with the large bison. Watch out for those horns, Jim."

Jim didn't say much, but it's difficult to be chatty when you're suffocating. Mostly, he just gave Marlin a look that said, "Why don't you either do something useful or drop dead?"

I got the straight scoop on the making of at least one show. A good friend of mine (we'll call him Scotty) was up in northern Minnesota, ostensibly trapping and tagging timber wolves for the Forest Service to determine numbers of animals, how far they ranged, etc.

In my opinion, he'd found a perfect excuse to hole up in a line shack and eat pickled eggs and beef jerky and drink beer all day—but I digress. He came into camp one day to stock up on provisions (beer, jerky, etc.), and found the "Wild Kingdom" film crew there with Marlin, Jim, and the gang. They were supposedly looking for bobcats.

Anyhow, while Scotty watched, they set up all the cameras and filmed Marlin and Jim blasting through the woods on snowmobiles.

Now, bobcats are fairly reclusive animals, and they aren't much for noisy, crowded parties, so I suspect the closest living animal may actually have been somewhere in Wisconsin. No problem. It was a beautiful, sunny day, and Marlin jumped off his machine and pointed his finger in a wide, sweeping arc.

Next, they inserted some file footage of a big cat loping through the woods in the middle of a blinding snowstorm. Back to Marlin and Jim in the sunshine, who vaulted onto their sleds just like the L.R. and Tonto and, with a hearty,

"Heigh-ho, Polaris," took off in hot pursuit of the alleged animal.

I don't recall how it ended, but Jim probably required 30 to 40 stitches, a couple of units of whole blood, and a bit of reconstructive surgery on his face: "Watch out for those claws, Jim..."

Salmon Fervor

Picture this: You roll out of bed at 4:30 a.m., chow down on some bacon and eggs, and you and all your neighbors stroll out to the curb, facing each other across the street in the middle of a driving rainstorm.

Then, at dawn, you all start lobbing rocks and firing slingshots back and forth across the street. Sounds dreadful, you say? That's OK. You might be happier as a golfer or, perhaps, a bowler. But if you responded, "cool" to the above scenario, you may have what it takes to be a salmon fisherman.

Every year, when thousands of king salmon scurry up the Lake Michigan tributaries in search of last-gasp love and romance, the same waters are invaded by a horde of quasi-sportsman meat mongers (the Michigan equivalent of an Alaskan brown bear with a hangover).

The sleepy little town of Hesperia, on the banks of the White River, has a nice waterfall hole that's slightly larger than your neighbor's swimming pool. It's the perfect place for a couple of friends to spend the afternoon fishing, and it can accommodate five or six guys if they're polite and careful not to intrude into their neighbors' air/water space.

Well, picture 38 fishermen (I counted) standing shoulder to shoulder, while 30 more are waiting on deck like airplanes stacked up over O'Hare. Every one of these guys is armed with a monstrous fishing rod with all the tender whip of a pool cue, a reel with 200 yards of monofilament line that could beach a mako shark, and a net large enough for a sumo wrestler.

The fun begins at first light, when they all start flinging heavily weighted flies, spawn bags, and treble hooks back and forth past each other's ears. Every one of these rigs is accompanied by three or four ounces of lead shot, so they might just as well be firing muzzle loaders at each other.

A wise man (my cousin Kup) once said, "Never underestimate the potential of high-speed monofilament." Some guys get bonked by their neighbors' rigs, while others are snagged in their now-leaking waders. Others, after getting snarled up on the bottom, lean back full force on their fishing rods, only to have the bait pop free, and a quarter-pound of 120 mph lead shot nails them right between the eyes.

Everyone is waving fishing rods and bobbing and weaving to avoid being hit, so the whole scene looks like some sort of weird, redneck ballet. Finally, someone at the very top of the hole gets into 25 pounds of angry salmon, and the fish tears off downstream, tangling 20 lines in the process. Everyone yells, "Fish on!" and it's only one fish.

If the Keystone Cops had made a fishing movie, this would be it.

The whole process becomes even more entertaining when you consider that most of these guys aren't up early; they're up late.

Consider Bubba, who has just been ushered out of the local tavern at 2 a.m., was driven (somehow) home for a nightcap (or three) until 4 a.m., pounded down four eggs and a pound of sausage links (which, by the way, aren't getting along so well with his last Boilermaker), and now crawls into his waders and heads for the river.

Now, picture 30 such Bubbas, each one hung over, with breath like an outhouse, waders leaking, surly, grouchy, and standing shoulder to shoulder with the same idiot that spilled a pitcher of beer on him three hours before.

So, if you want to enjoy the beauty and serenity of nature, maybe take a walk in the woods. But if you enjoy watching dysfunctional groups of people participating in tag team sports, go check out your local salmon hole.

Buffalo Bob Bothers Bison

Bison should come with a warning label. "Caution: Prolonged exposure to this creature may result in being stomped."

I've spent a fairly significant amount of time slogging around Yellowstone country in pursuit of the wily trout and so have logged a number of hours in fairly close proximity to these big beasts (bison, not trout).

The problem is, they look like big, slow, stuffed animals, so the tourists think they can take liberties with them. *Helpful Hint:* Cow-tipping doesn't work with bison.

Anyhow, here's a rundown of a few close encounters.

The most ridiculous one I ever saw was in the Madison River area, where a group of four or five bison was bedded down in a meadow. Some city-boy father wanted to get a picture, so he ventured out to within about 30 feet, and then instructed his son (probably 10 or so) to pitch a rock at an animal to get it to stand up.

Well, it worked.

The kid turned loose a pretty sharp chunk of slate, and it popped the big boy right on the snout (the bison, not the dad). The bison literally vaulted into a charge position and feigned a short burst in dad's direction.

There was a little poetic justice that day. The boy (unscathed) covered the hundred yards back to the camper faster than Usain Bolt. However, the dad (scathed), got a little ahead of his feet and did a lovely chin plant on a very rocky section of ground. This situation was exacerbated by the fate of his $800 camera lens, which broke not only his fall, but two or three ribs as well, and would later require some assembly to return to its original condition (the lens <u>and</u> the dad).

The last I saw, the guy was hobbling back to camp, cursing and bleeding profusely from the mouth.

If you're at Fishing Bridge, you can cross the bridge, make an immediate right onto a gravel service road, and then another immediate right onto a concrete boat launch that extends down into the river. It's a great place to eat lunch and watch the trout feed.

One day, as I walked up the service road toward the bridge, I observed a park ranger making a presentation to a large group of happy campers on the boat launch. Just as I reached the bridge, I saw a large bull bison jogging across directly at me, and I immediately backed off.

So, why did the bison cross the bridge? To have some fun on the other side.

The old boy cruised across the bridge (ignoring me), made the right onto the service road, and then did a <u>big</u> swooping head fake in the direction of the tourists on the ramp.

It was a thing of beauty. The whole gaggle (ranger included) took their only option, and 20 people found themselves bathing in the Yellowstone River. They looked as though they'd been washed off a pier. His job done, the bison continued up the service road.

I think I heard him chuckling.

My own close encounter happened in the Lamar River valley. I'd fished for three or four hours, skirting some bison that were too close to the river for comfort (they're bothersome if hooked with one's back cast), and found myself about two miles from the car in the late afternoon.

Storms seem to come out of nowhere in the mountains, and a real whopper of a thunderstorm rolled in before I had a chance to take cover. The sky opened up, and I beat feet for the only stand of trees in the area.

I got there at about the time the rain turned to hail, so I hunkered down against a tree in the high grass, pulled my vest up over my head, and waited it out. It was dark and hailing and the wind was howling, and I'd been there almost 20 minutes with no end in sight.

Suddenly, I heard a low groan, which I figured was just a tree in the wind. Then, I smelled a rather rank, musty odor, so I stood up in the high grass and found myself about 20 feet from a <u>very</u> large bull that was facing directly at me. The whole herd had wandered in to take refuge, and there were bison everywhere.

Apparently, this town wasn't big enough for the both of us, and the big boy grumbled again and took a couple steps directly at me. I had this awful vision of being gored like a rodeo clown or impaled against my tree, so I jumped up, yelling and waving my arms, and he stopped.

Finally, he changed course and wandered over to lie down about 50 yards away. I scrambled out the back way, as the hail was finally letting up, and found a less-populated place to fish. Stupid bison.

Biking: A (Cult)ural Tour

For the past several years, a number of my body parts (knees, Achilles' tendons, etc.) have been sending me not-so-subtle messages that maybe it's time to run a bit less and find alternative ways to stay in shape.

So, this past spring, I bought a road bike. I had a visual image of casual rides up the rail trail on a perfect fall afternoon with the birds singing, the leaves in blazing color, and people smiling, just like those commercials for feminine hygiene products.

Unfortunately, I appear to have fallen in with the wrong crowd.

Two good friends of mine (we'll call them Tom and Beth) are experienced bikers, and they invited me to join them for a ride. This got to be a regular thing, until finally we stretched it far enough to include a bakery visit at our favorite place about 13 miles north of here.

At one of these stops, while eating apple fritters and slurping chocolate milk, Tom suggested that we should consider doing this way cool bike tour up near Traverse City. It was presented as just a fun ride, not a race, where you can go at your own pace and enjoy the scenery. The course, as I understood it, had "a few rolling hills." You know, like the Alps.

I think this is how cult leaders operate.

They sound so honest and reasonable, and you find yourself smiling and nodding and being totally sucked in to whatever they're selling. It seems even more plausible when they tag-team you with another member who says how great it sounds to her, too. Waco, here I come.

So, we arrived at this little shindig at about 7:30 in the morning and found a parking lot full of remnants from the Tour de France. These people had aerodynamic helmets and pedals with toe clips and padded gloves and fancy shirts with pockets in the back to store bananas and cardboard-flavored energy bars.

I should have run away screaming, but my cult leader(s) assured me that everything would be fine. They always say that.

We met two brothers (we'll call them Ben and George) who planned to join us for the ride. Ben looked like me, a convert-in-training, and seemed a little worried about what was to transpire. George was apparently one of the cult's lieutenants, and he had that crazed look in his eye (like a rabid raccoon or the president of Iran) that said he'd rather hurtle down a narrow mountain road than win the lottery.

So, we all started out on a ride that was farther than from Denver to Colorado Springs, but at least I'd been promised a relaxed, pedestrian pace on gentle hills. Sure.

After a couple miles of easy cruising, we rounded a bend and came to the base of what could only be described as Pike's Peak. You could have fallen off this thing. It went straight up for almost a mile, and just when it appeared to finally end, it turned right and did it all again. We were in danger of being struck by low-flying aircraft.

Well, what goes up…

So, with a scant 10 seconds to recover at the top (I heard someone ask whether anyone had seen his lung), we began a semi-controlled free fall to the bottom at speeds usually associated with the Bonneville Salt Flats.

George was smiling. He had bugs in his teeth.

Then, just when I thought I could finally relax, we ran into a few of their demented friends and formed a drafting line designed to make us go faster. Swell. The lead guy pedals like mad, while those behind ride in the slipstream about four centimeters off each other's wheels, just like a flock of geese.

There is no daydreaming during this process, because total concentration is required not to bump somebody and bring them all down in a heap. I didn't see any scenery, just shoes and an assortment of spandex-adorned rear ends. If this isn't considered racing, I've been misinformed for all these years.

Finally, we reached the first of three aid stations, an oasis in the wilderness. The soup was wonderful. I didn't want to leave. Somehow, I survived four segments of this madness and made it to the finish line, my legs protesting every inch the way. They still haven't spoken to me.

I hear there's another of these little parties in a couple weeks. Perhaps you should consider it. It's nice and flat, and we're just going to ride an easy, comfortable pace. Ours should be a pretty good-size group, with Tom and Beth and Ben and George and several old colleagues of David Koresh.

Nordic Skiing: People in Wacky Suits

For those of you who might be bowlers or golfers, there's a small segment of the population that spends its winter weekends driving all over the northern states in search of Nordic (cross-country) ski races.

There aren't many events in this neck of the woods, because we can't seem to keep snow on the ground long enough to enjoy it, but the north end of Michigan's mitt has some really cool happenings.

Those who participate would cite the beauty of our forests, the chance to commune with nature, the advantages of total body fitness, and other meaningful reasons for getting involved in this sport. Actually, it's just the perfect excuse to wear clothing that you couldn't wear to the office (or to a tavern in rural Luther).

Imagine your middle-aged body in a waterproof, one-piece, skin-tight, chartreuse and fluorescent blue racing suit, and you know what I'm talking about. Toss in a pair of red and yellow racing boots and some wrap-around shades, and the ensemble is complete.

Regardless of whether you're an elite racer or a recreational participant, the cast of characters alone is worth the price of admission.

At a recent event, I was entertained by some rather quirky individuals. The first was probably an ex-lifeguard, perhaps during the Nixon era. He made his entrance into the registration area like he was walking on stage to accept an Oscar. A hush fell over the crowd. He had long, curly hair which flowed back in a distinctive (and disturbing) mullet. The color, a little tough to describe, was a peculiar orange-blonde shade that made me wonder if there'd been an accident with a can of Franco-American spaghetti.

His face sported the best tan that money could buy, and his finally sculpted figure (which reminded me a little of Jim Belushi's) was packed into a powder blue racing suit that was three sizes too small and accentuated every roll and protrusion—every protrusion.

Imagine the Lone Ranger on a steady diet of beer and French fries, and you get the picture. It was really quite stunning. Anyhow, he walked in and circulated around the room several times, just to make sure we all noticed him. We did.

The start of the race was organized pandemonium. Picture a running race with hundreds of people packed in shoulder to shoulder. Now strap boards to their feet. Now arm them with a couple of razor-sharp javelins. The possibilities are endless.

Theoretically, everyone should double-pole out cautiously to avoid contact with his neighbor, but there's always one fool who didn't get the memo. In our case, it was the lifeguard.

The gun went off, and he started skating and flailing like a windmill in a hurricane. So, five seconds into the race, a dozen people went down in a giant yard sale of arms and legs and poles and skis that looked like the aftermath of a tsunami. Luckily, I slid by unscathed.

Once on course, I encountered another interesting individual. To say the least, he was unhappy.

I don't know whether he had the wrong wax, or his underwear was too tight, or maybe he was just having a bad day. Regardless, a couple miles up the trail, we were all going by him like he was a stump in the river. I was in a line of eight or nine people who were politely passing him in single file. Each skier would say, "On your left," as a courtesy before he went by. Usually you get a pleasant response, but this jerk was livid.

At first, he actually tried to block the lane and prevent us from passing. Then, as each of us went by, he gave a nasty scowl and a stream of #&%#*%@ expletives that wasn't suitable for tender ears. I don't think he was enjoying his wilderness experience.

The last guy worthy of mention was a very good skier, certainly faster than I was, but gravity was his literally his downfall. He was about 50 yards ahead of me when he came to a long downhill.

There's a law of physics which says that an object in motion will tend to stay in motion along a straight line unless influenced by an external force, such as a tree. (OK, I'm paraphrasing.) Anyhow, at the bottom of the hill, the trail made a hard right, and he didn't.

Last I saw, he was cartwheeling about 20 yards into the woods. A few minutes later, here he came again, looking like the Abominable Snowman. He pulled up next to me and said hello just as we crested a short, steep hill. On the way down, he stepped into the parallel track used by classic skiers. Bad idea.

The problem is, once you're in the track, it's not easy to get out of the track.

This time the trail made a hard left. His skis stayed in the groove, but his upper body again proceeded straight along the tangent, and he made a beautiful swan dive into a cedar bush. That was the last time I saw him.

So, are you up to a new challenge? Maybe it's time to dust off the old boards, try to locate an Eric Heiden racing suit on eBay, and hit the road for parts north.

Chapter 4

People are Weird

Each of us is unique. That's a nice, politically correct way to say that we're all a little quirky, eccentric, bizarre, or just plain goofy. Still, it's these oddities that make life so entertaining.

A Day at Mirdle Beach

When you hear the word "myrtle," you probably think of the green, leafy groundcover that's better than grass in some shady areas. Well, there's a new myrtle in town, and it's spelled "mirdle," as in, "brand new, by gosh, women's underwear for men."

I looked it up, and this new male underwear/girdle garment is being marketed by an Australian company as shape wear or compression wear for paunchy, middle-aged men who sit at a desk all day and don't go to the gym. It sounds as though you can skip the workout, eat a dozen jelly doughnuts, and still look like Johnny Weissmuller—as long as you're wearing your mirdle (but not a loincloth, please).

In fact, this company is going way out on a limb, suggesting that these new, male elastic wonder pants may actually improve your circulation and lower your golf score. Good luck with that one. I suppose if you cinch that gut in far enough to actually see the ball, there should be some benefit. However, for most of us, the best way to post a better score is to just quit after the seventh hole.

I find this whole thing a bit creepy and bothersome on several fronts. The first is the "How do I get started?" concept.

Let's say you're a middle-aged businessman with a 44-inch waist and 30 or 40 pounds of love handles. If you come into work on Monday wearing a pair of size 29/32 Dockers, someone is going to notice, and the comments might not be what you'd hoped for.

Second, there is a law of physics stating that mass is neither created nor destroyed. In lay terms, this means that it has to go *somewhere*.

If you buy a mirdle and squash that waist in to look like a teenage boy, all that flab just gets relocated. I'm thinking up. The result will look like a pushup bra gone bad, with the wearer sporting big man breasts and huge underarm flab, reminiscent of the phormer physique of a phamous leftie golfer.

Third, from a purely practical standpoint, what happens when, as is typical for middle-aged men, you need to use the restroom five or six times during the workday? How long does it take to wrestle in and out of an elastic straitjacket? What happens when the air conditioning goes on the fritz at the office and your entire torso is wrapped in Neoprene? You'd better invest in some industrial-strength antiperspirant.

Fourth, do you remember Janet Jackson's wardrobe malfunction at the Super Bowl? Kid stuff. What happens when a crucial seam on this thing gets stretched to the limit and decides to blow? Some poor, innocent bystander could be walking down the street, minding his own business, and suddenly be nailed by a projectile undergarment doing Mach 3.

Finally, what about truth in advertising? Let's say that, thanks to your new, gorgeous figure, you find yourself in the company of a beautiful 30-something high-maintenance woman who decides you're the man of her dreams.

Maybe she wants to take the plunge and get married. Maybe she just wants to spend a romantic weekend at some exotic beach resort. Either way, a time will come when you'll have to shed the mirdle, and the real you (all that mass that wasn't destroyed, only displaced) will return to its original coordinates. It won't be a pretty sight. The supermodel will probably leave skid marks.

Just Humor Me

Ever since the '50s, hundreds of people claim to have been abducted by alien invaders, taken aboard spaceships, transported to distance galaxies, and then returned more or less intact.

Most of these reports have been viewed as hoaxes, the hallucinations of cable freaks watching too many reruns of "Star Trek" or "Lost in Space."

Why would these aliens want us? Are they obsessed with human blood? Do they take us to some secret laboratory and perform unmentionable experiments? If so, why would they bother to return us? Is it a sport, like trout fishing, where they're required to catch and release?

These questions have remained unanswered—until now.

It's my theory that these aliens are taking a random sample of human beings across the globe, surgically removing their funny bones, and then releasing them back into the general population. So, although they might *look* like the rest of us, they no longer fit into normal society, as they have no sense of humor whatsoever.

I first came across this phenomenon while working at an engineering firm up north. The guys I worked with were a decent bunch, but one of them (we'll call him Dennis) didn't have even a hint of humor in his entire being. Not a smirk. Not a chortle. I didn't think it was possible.

The rest of us would be telling jokes or doing Three Stooges imitations and generally yukking it up, and poor Dennis would be sitting in his chair with this expressionless Stepford Wife look on his face. The more we laughed, the more stoical he became. I've seen bald eagles that look happier.

Do you remember the old "Make Me Laugh" show? Essentially, the contestants had to sit in a chair while professional comedians did sight gags and anything else they could dream up to make them laugh. ("What is it about riding in a car alone that makes you pick your nose?")

Anyhow, getting ol' Dennis to chuckle became our mission in life, so we kept ramping up our presentations, using our best stuff—everything from elephant jokes to armpit noises—and still nothing. Just that blank look.

I recall one morning when he came in looking particularly surly. I asked what was wrong, and he said, "I told the wife, I said, 'You'd better have the dinner on the table when I get home.'"

Lots of his sentences began with, "I told the wife, I said….."

Well, I couldn't let that just lie there, so I asked him, real serious like, if that meant the food had to be hot in the pan and ready to serve when he arrived, or if it actually had to be on his plate and properly cooled, so he could walk through the door, slide into his chair, and start eating immediately.

No response. Nothing. The other guys were rolling on the floor.

In retrospect, it just never occurred to me that he might have been the victim of some terrible alien experiment.

So, do you have a close friend or relative who concerns you? Someone who will never get to wear the uniform of the Good Humor Man? If so, how can you tell if he's the victim of some alien prank or just naturally as dull as Al Gore?

The answer is easy. Simply go out and rent the entire Pink Panther series, with Peter Sellers as Chief Inspector Jacques Clouseau, and watch as he takes Commissioner Charles Dreyfus to the brink of insanity. Sit your friend down, and observe the master as he attempts to fix the phone, or poses as a dentist and pulls the wrong tooth, or as a Swedish pirate with a leaky inflatable parrot.

No true human being can stand up to this kind of barrage, no matter how serious he is.

If, after watching all this, he merely gives you a blank stare and says, "I told the wife, I said, 'You'd better make the popcorn,'" you should first check for pods, and then get away as soon as you can—before it happens to you.

The Skinny on Skinny Jeans

Do you have a driver's license? Take it out; I'll wait.

OK, now examine it carefully. If it says you were born before 2000, or you are male, then you probably have no business wearing a pair of today's newfangled (I like that word) skinny jeans.

Actually, gotcha! My opening line was a trick question. If you have a driver's license, you're already too long in the tooth to wear a pair.

While on campus the other day, I saw a young man literally staggering along. He looked to be in pain. My first impression was that he was wearing a cast, but the culprit turned out to be his brand new sprayed-on pants. He, like many of his peers, had obviously discovered really tasty and unlimited cafeteria food and may have added his "freshman 16" in kilograms.

That's no crime, but we should all dress according to our size and body type. His fashion faux pas was trying to pack himself into a pair of pants that would have been snug on a 10-year-old girl.

The problem is that, if you squeeze 200 pounds of sausage into a 100-pound casing, the rest has to go *somewhere.* Therefore, if you don't have the physique to comfortably wear these stupid things, you either end up with 14-inch cankles or a spare tire that could fit a farm tractor.

On the positive side, if you go boating, you won't need a life vest, but that's only a minor advantage.

The other issue is circulation, or the lack of it. After a few hours of wearing one of these double-barreled tourniquets, you'll be working on an early case of gangrene and soon will be stumbling around like Boris Karloff in "Frankenstein." That would explain my college student sighting.

Interestingly, skinny jeans have actually been around since the '70s. No, really. The first practitioner was a 40-something-year-old Yooper who lived in Covington and worked on a construction crew. I think his name was Jimmy. The guy was about six feet tall and somewhere in the vicinity of 412 pounds of finely sculpted PBR and cheeseburgers.

Anyhow, he was a man mountain, with massive arms and shoulders and a neck like a bull. He could have changed a tire on his Ford pickup without using a jack. He wore the same old XXXXXXXL flannel shirt every day, and a pair of what looked like 29-26 jeans that ran out of room about halfway to his waist. I suspect he purchased them in junior high.

As a result, there were about two acres of exposed ham protruding out the back, and an enormous belly hoisted up and hanging over the front. That was when he was standing up. When he bent over to work, well, never mind. I'm just glad I'm not a proctologist.

Unfortunately, I'm afraid that Jimmy, fashion visionary that he was, never got a patent on his idea, and someone else is enjoying all the gravy. I just thought you should know their true origin.

I'm not sure where fashion will go from here. Shorts have gone from actual shorts to pedal pushers to, well, pants. Pants have gotten so tight that they only fit members of Undereaters Anonymous.

What's next? Trousers with the fly in the back? Neckties worn around the waist? I think I'll buy up a couple thousand Nehru jackets on eBay and make a killing when they come back into vogue.

Hans Was a Flying Buff

Hold everything, and start changing your vacation plans.

A travel agency in Frankfurt, Germany, is now booking a unique flight from the town of Erfurt to the Baltic Sea resort of Usedom. What makes it so special, you ask?

Why, as it turns out, it's the first-of-its-kind trial nudist flight.

Now, it wasn't clear (at least to me) whether it was a flight for trial nudists or a trial flight for nudists, so I'll leave that for greater minds to ponder. Regardless, passengers will be required to keep it under wraps until they board the plane, and the flight crew must remain fully clothed for safety reasons, whatever the heck that means.

One could argue that if all people were required to fly naked, the entire check-in process would be drastically streamlined, as there would be no need for metal detectors and passenger frisking.

Sorry, I'm not buying it. During the Second World War, the Nazis banned nudism, but it picked up again after Uncle Adolf cashed in his chips. Well, at least he had one good idea. The last thing the world needs is a bunch of middle-aged naked people.

In my opinion, there's a reason why Baby Boomers wear clothes. Basically, since middle-class civilians like us lack the financial resources to get expensive cosmetic enhancements, there is very little similarity between our bodies and those purchased by Angelina Jolie or Brad Pitt. They have six-pack abs and perky protrusions. The rest of us have unsightly blemishes and a sagging economy.

Still, because beauty is in the eye, as it were, let's consider the implications of stripping all the clothing off your "Body by Knockwurst" physique and flying cross-country in your birthday suit.

First, nobody likes sitting in a cramped airplane when the guy next to you is infringing on your personal space. So picture, if you will, how pleasant it would be if you were stuck (literally) in the middle seat between Larry the Cable Guy and Jabba the Hutt. Now picture the same scenario if both of them were as naked as the day they were born (or in Jabba's case, hatched). Kinda makes you lose your appetite, huh?

In addition, let's just consider the complications that could arise from passengers traveling in this condition. The drink selection would certainly have to be limited.

Caffeinated beverages would definitely be out. The last thing these people need is a stimulant. Likewise, alcohol seems like a bad idea. Do we really want them lowering their inhibition levels even further? And then there's hot coffee, which, when mixed with cream and sugar and a little turbulence, could be a real disaster. I think that leaves only Tang.

Finally, when I fly, I'm never all that thrilled about using one of those little pillows they issue you, because I'm not sure whose Brylcreem-covered scalp was the last to use it, or when it (the scalp, not the pillow) was last shampooed. So, putting this as delicately as possible, I'm quite sure that I wouldn't care to be snuggled up in a seat on that airline's next flight after it had been occupied by a colony of flabby nudists.

Maybe I'm just a bit old-fashioned, but couldn't they just keep their parts covered until they get to the beach?

I've Lost My ... Hoover

Are you familiar with "Catch-22"?

Yes, it's a book, and also a pretty good movie, but do you remember the actual catch? If memory serves, the premise is that you can get out of the military if you're crazy, but you have to request a competency test. If you're rational enough to waltz in and ask for a psychological evaluation, you must not be crazy after all, so you can't get out.

Similarly, the problem with losing one's glasses is that, in order to find one's glasses, one must be wearing one's glasses (hereafter known as Catch-20/20).

Have you lost anything lately, perhaps your wallet, your purse, your keys, your lunch, your way, your temper, your luggage, your grip, your marbles, your place, or your train of thought? I don't suppose I tend to misplace things any more often than the next guy, but I seem to go in streaks, much like a wide receiver who suddenly (and inexplicably) drops five in a row.

As a first-grader growing up in Grand Rapids, I walked to school every day (five miles uphill each way through three feet of snow—no, wait, that's another story). Anyhow, I always carried my lunch and milk money, which was probably only 10 or 15 cents.

It didn't matter, because every day I would arrive, and the money would be missing—as gone as Jimmy Hoffa or socks in the dryer. This went on for weeks. I still have no idea where the money (or Jimmy) went, but I'm thinking of finding a couple of those guys who investigate cold cases and turning them loose on it.

After a week or so of this nonsense, my mom got fed up and started putting the money in an envelope, which went in my pants pocket. So, for the next week or so I'd arrive at school, only to discover that the money and the envelope had disappeared. The Amazing Kreskin couldn't have topped it.

So—we're not done yet—my mom finally put the money in an envelope, which went in a brown shopping bag, which I looked pretty stupid carrying to school, and the very first time I arrived...well, it staggers the imagination. I'm thinking poltergeists or some alien space creature with a warped sense of humor.

Much later, in my middle twenties, while living in the Upper Peninsula, I was cleaning out the car with our nice, new Hoover vacuum cleaner. It's a little fuzzy, but as I reconstruct the scene of the crime, I believe I finished vacuuming the driver side floor, set the vacuum on the roof while I cleaned out the glove box, suddenly remembered something I needed in town, and hit the road.

That was the last time we saw our poor little Hoover.

Upon my return home, my wife inquired as to its location, and I spent the next half-hour combing the bushes between Houghton and Atlantic Mine. Nothing.

If that wasn't embarrassing enough, we decided to call the local radio station and put it on the Lost and Found list (which was broadcast to the population three or four times a day). You can picture the announcer, having gotten through the usual list of dogs and cats and what not, suddenly encountering, "Lost: a standard-size Hoover vacuum cleaner (*chuckle*) somewhere in the ditch between Houghton and (*chuckle*) Atlantic Mine. If found, please call the following number..."

We had people calling our house just to find out what kind of idiot could lose a 20-pound piece of equipment the size of a golf bag. Apparently, the same kind that could lose his milk money—in an envelope, in a brown paper bag.

Needless to say, Hoover was never heard from again. I only hope it found a good home.

Better Nev Than Later

I've always been a fairly prompt person.

Perhaps it's just my internal clock or my upbringing or whatever, but if we're invited to dinner at 7 p.m., I consider "fashionably late" to be somewhere around 7:05.

A dear friend of ours was getting married in Leland a few weeks ago, with a rather simple, but elegant outdoor ceremony planned in the garden area adjacent to the house. The whole GFO (Gala Festive Occasion) would start at 5 p.m. on Friday.

Mind you, this friend is one of the funniest people I've ever met, generous to a fault, and someone who just loves a good excuse to mercilessly tease her closest friends. Hence, it's not wise to give her any ammunition.

The Friday traffic promised to be heavy, so we left a half-hour early to be sure we arrived on time. Unfortunately, this wasn't enough.

As we headed west off 131, the lakes area in Cadillac looked like a big, long parking lot. We found ourselves about 212th in a line of cars and boat trailers and campers and RVs stretched out like a wagon train, and all bottled up at one nasty light that turns green just long enough to allow six vehicles to bolt through.

After about 20 minutes, it was obvious that our cushion was gone and we simply weren't going to make it. I reacted in my usual rational and professional manner—by screaming &%$#@*$& expletives, honking the horn, slamming my fist on the steering wheel, and generally doing my impression of a New York cabbie.

Once through the light, I figured we still had an outside chance of making it, assuming all the planets were properly aligned and the Red Sea parted to provide us an open road. Not likely.

In retrospect, there must have been some sort of Sunday drivers convention planned for Traverse City that weekend, as we found ourselves behind an endless line of retirees doing 43 MPH amid a giant convoy of minivans. The only plus was that we were getting great gas mileage.

Anyway, we were still about 15 miles out when the ceremony was due to start, so we had a number of choices. The first was simply to arrive late and try to sneak in unnoticed. The second was to avoid embarrassment, stop for a cold drink, skip the wedding entirely, and arrive in time for the reception. The third was to throw ourselves on the mercy of the court and claim some extraordinary excuse, like alien abduction or our alarm clock didn't go off.

Hoping that the blessed event would simply start a little late, we opted for choice No. 1. We parked out on the road and tiptoed in on the gravel drive. I figured we had a pretty good chance of sliding in undetected until Jan whispered, "Uh oh, this can't be good."

I looked up and discovered that we'd landed center stage, with the bride and groom, the members of the wedding party, and all of the distinguished guests facing (and looking) directly at us. To make matters worse, the bride (whose face only we and the minister could see) was obviously trying to stifle a belly laugh, and I was sure she was going to throw up her arms, stop the ceremony, and announce, "Well, look who's here!" or, "Ladies and gentlemen, may I introduce our third choice for Best Man and Matron of Honor?"

That she managed to ignore us was almost worse, like when your father tells you, "Just wait until we get home," and you know there's a great discomfort planned for your near future.

The long and short of it was that, even though all the guests probably thought we were rude, the bride claimed she still loves us and said our embarrassment was the nicest wedding gift we could have given her. She opened it right away, and teased us mercilessly during the reception.

My protests of, "The traffic was horrendous," and, "But we left a half-hour early," only added fuel to an already roaring fire.

I finally just shut up.

The Great Dating Disaster

A friend of mine (we'll call her Laura) is a single mom employed as a clerical worker and receptionist in a busy college campus office.

She's the first smiling face you see when you walk in. When you enter, she's facing the door, her nameplate prominently displayed on her desk. To her right, on the wall, is an arrangement of business cards from everyone in the office complex.

So, a couple of weeks back, a student walked in and needed some help. She got him the necessary information and directed him to an office elsewhere in the building. He seemed confused, so she offered to escort him to his destination. Before leaving, she asked her colleague (we'll call her Meredith) to take over at the desk until she returned.

Well, as they walked, it became obvious that the young man was interested, and he stammered and flirted a bit and finally asked whether he could take her to lunch. She countered that she was a mother of two and likely not in his age bracket. He pulled out the old "age is only a number" cliché, and blah, blah, blah.

Anyhow, she said she'd think about it, and given that they hadn't even exchanged names, she figured the point was moot. Not so.

The guy (Matt) was pretty resourceful. A few days later she got a text message from him (obviously, he'd grabbed her card) suggesting that they should get together.

She said no thanks. He persisted, saying he was in town that day and that they could have lunch up the street, not a date, no expectations, just lunch. So, she finally agreed, and he described his car and offered to pick her up in front of the building.

So, at noon, she walked out, hopped in, and realized that he somehow looked different. Well, it had been a couple of weeks. They had lunch, and in that hour she decided that it wasn't meant to be. First, he was overly opinionated. Second, he was 23. As she put it, "If I'd been a promiscuous 14-year-old, I could have been his mother."

At least it was a free lunch, and on the way back he said, "By the way, I love what you've done with your hair." She looked puzzled, and asked what he meant. He said, "You know, the dark brown color." She replied, "I'm Italian. It's always been this color."

Yes, folks, it was then and only then that both of them realized they had never before set eyes on each other.

The young man whom she had delivered upstairs was gone forever. Matt had met Meredith, a very blonde woman who looks more Swedish than Italian. He saw the nameplate (on the desk where Meredith was sitting temporarily), picked up Laura's card, contacted her, and the rest is dating history.

How this could have happened is still a mystery (at least to me). Are they both in need of new eyeglasses? Was there a patch of patchy dense fog in the car? Are they both missing a cognitive gene?

Regardless, our heroine walked out of her building and got into a car on a busy downtown street with a complete stranger. I've changed the names so her mother doesn't find out. Actually, I get it from the guy's perspective. If you're single, and a pretty girl wants to jump in your car and join you for lunch, why fight it?

Unfortunately, the person lost in this unlikely conundrum (I like that word) is poor Meredith. For her, there is no new love and romance, no free lunch, and no impending nuptials (I like that word, too). Matt continues to send rambling text messages to Laura in spite of her efforts to unload the little twerp.

Will Matt finally realize that Laura isn't Swedish? Will love finally blossom for Meredith? Will the fog ever lift? Find out in next week's thrilling episode of "The Young and the Rest of Us."

Just Call Me Muffin

I finally hit my limit this past weekend.

Normally, I just smile and ignore it, but in the past two days I made purchases in three establishments, and the cashiers called me "hon" in all three. I suppose if my name was Attila, I could understand this, but my driver's license says otherwise.

There seem to be three major phases in a person's life. In the first one, you're a cute little tyke, and women (especially aunts and your parents' friends) just love to call you honey or their little angel and pinch your (upper) cheeks. So, you smile and deal with it, try to bob and weave and stay at arm's length, and figure you got off lucky if some great aunt didn't manage to plant a big, old, ruby-red, sloppy one on your forehead.

In the second phase, your ego gets an occasional boost if some attractive person gives you a kind word or warm smile, or perhaps a second look that (you imagine) says, "Hey, sweetie, maybe we ought to get acquainted." Even if you're married or have a significant other, it's occasionally nice to discover that you aren't totally invisible.

Then, there's Phase Three.

The bothersome thing is that I may have unknowingly entered it without any fanfare or formal announcement. The problem is, you still think you're in Phase Two. So, when you look across the room and see an attractive woman smiling in your direction, you fail to realize that it's because your fly is open.

Phase Three is when, especially to 20- or 30-something women, you no longer pose any sort of threat or generate any more interest than yesterday's meatloaf. Somehow, you find yourself in a big warehouse of middle-aged and older people who are once again treated like their Phase One days (pinched cheeks, pet names like "sweetie" and "hon"), and there appears to be no way out.

We had a very lovely and perceptive exchange student in our home who, on her first trip to the bank to open an account, was called "hon" or "sweetie" seven times in five minutes. I wasn't paying much attention, but she counted.

Afterward, in the car, she said: "I don't understand all these names you people call each other. Everyone is *sweetie* and *honey* and *pumpkin* and *muffin*."

So, when I asked why that was so bad, she informed me that pumpkins are big and round and orange, and muffins are full of fat. *Touché.*

I haven't decided what to do about my own phase three dilemma. I suppose I could dye my hair jet black to try to look younger, but I fear I might resemble James Arness in that remake of "Gunsmoke." (His hair looked like a cross between a beaver pelt and a Beatles wig.)

My other choice is to seek out cashiers and sales people in their eighties, because I probably still look like a youngster to them, but then I risk getting my cheeks pinched.

Meanwhile, the next person who says, "Thanks, hon," is going to get, "You're welcome, pumpkin," in return.

I hope all of you sweet little muffins have a nice day.

Express Yourself

There's a 1980s song by Madonna called "Express Yourself."

I never gave the concept much thought, until recently I was gabbing with an old friend, and she was telling me about her daughter's dog.

As the story goes, the daughter in question (we'll call her Emily) is tighter than Jack Benny and, in an effort to save a few pesos, normally performs most routine grooming operations herself. However, the dog (we'll call him Fido) was exhibiting behavior that was, well, socially unacceptable.

Picture hosting a dinner shindig for a few close friends, and just as you're hauling out the wine and appetizers, Fido comes butt-surfing through the dining room, dragging himself with his front legs. Suddenly, the guacamole doesn't seem quite so appealing.

So, Emily took the pooch to a groomer, who, for $65 gave him the super-duper deluxe treatment. We're talking haircut, pedicure, bathing, and expressing his anal glands. This explains why my barber charges me only $13.

Anyhow, Emily felt compelled to describe this procedure in great detail to her mother over the phone while mom was finishing a bowl of oatmeal. As I understand it, most of it ended up in the disposal.

The groomer, aware of Emily's budget constraints, offered to give her a tutorial on where the glands are located and how to perform the procedure herself. For you do-it-yourself types, they're at 5 o'clock and 7 o'clock in that, uh, area. You have to get right up in there and squeeze the business end of the dog until, well, never mind. So, Emily got a firsthand lesson (literally) on how to express an anal gland.

As for myself, I'm thinking that certain tasks are best left to the professionals. These include such things as pumping out a septic tank, performing cataract surgery, removing a downed power line, and anything to do with the southern end of a north-facing canine.

I consider the groomer fee to be money well-spent, like the extra 10 bucks you pay to have your gas grill assembled. $65? Fine. I'd pay $165, but in return, I not only want the vet to perform the procedure, but I specifically don't want to know <u>any</u> of the graphic details thereof. Just call me when it's done.

However, perhaps you have a stronger constitution than I, and you wish to tackle this problem in-house. That is, take the dog by the tail and face the situation.

The good news is that there may be a couple of alternatives to doing the rubber glove thing yourself. The first is to take the dog to Emily's. She's a pro. The second is to find a neighbor with Berber carpet. It's nice and rough and might allow the dog to eliminate the problem on his own. Shag is just too soft to get the job done.

Before you invite yourself over for coffee, and this is important, you have to practice your routine in front of the mirror. You'll need to look completely <u>shocked</u> when the dog starts doing exactly what you took him over there to do. "Oh, Spike, now you just <u>stop</u> that. I'm so sorry, Mrs. Johnson. He's never done anything like this before. It must be that new food my husband gave him."

Yeah, sure. Unfortunately, one neighbor is probably good for only one visit, so you'll have to get acquainted with the whole block.

Expresso, uh, espresso, anyone?

Let's Raise a Glass to Diamond Jim

There's a character named Del Gue in the classic "Jeremiah Johnson" film (a nutso acquaintance of Robert Redford's) who shaves his head to make his scalp less attractive to the local hostiles. However, later in the movie, he re-grows a nice, thick mane, rationalizing that at least he could be remembered on some warrior's lodge pole.

Well, thanks to Algordanza, a small company in southeast Switzerland, you can keep your topknot and still achieve a level of immortality. They have the knowhow and the technology, and they are actually creating synthetic diamonds from the residual ashes of the dearly departed. No kidding.

My first impression was that this was kind of a novel idea. You could turn your spouse into a necklace, a nice pair of earrings, a stickpin, or even a naval piercing, if that's your thing. Heck, if this had been available 30 years ago, Mrs. Crosby could have transformed Bing into Bling.

The company marketing this venture suggests that your, uh, sparkling personality could even be mounted on your favorite table in the local pub. Until recently, the only alternative to a more traditional funeral was to have your ashes sprinkled over the Yellowstone River or the Appalachian Trail or wherever your heart called home. Unfortunately, you'd soon wash away downstream and end up in Lake Erie or some smelly place. Under the new plan, you'd never have to leave.

My second impression wasn't quite so romantic. In fact, the whole thing kinda creeps me out. First, they'd have to reduce you to nothing but carbon. It brings to mind some awful cereal I ate as a kid. What was that stuff? It had freeze-dried blueberries in it that looked like rabbit droppings, and they came to life when you added milk, much like lutefisk.

Next, they'd have to compress you under intense heat and pressure to create a diamond, as George Reeves used to do in the old '50s "Superman" series. Just the thought of it gives me a headache, and I'm thinking it'll be difficult to rest in peace with someone jamming me into a space smaller than a thimble.

Then, to top it all off, the living spouse gets to enjoy her twilight years in <u>really</u> close proximity to the couch potato who spent the last two decades channel surfing and snoring in her ear. So, no matter whether she's grocery shopping, playing pinochle with her friends, or even socializing with a new beau, there's old Diamond Jim, hanging around her neck and watching her every move. Maybe donating him to the pub isn't such a bad idea, after all.

Finally, they haven't been able to make a diamond larger than one carat, simply because we don't contain enough carbon to make something big and gaudy. So, if you really want to shine while being displayed dead-center (sorry) on your favorite table at Schuberg's Bar, you should probably take up residence there right now and start packing away the cheeseburgers and cold malt beverages.

With any luck, you could be a two-carat phenomenon.

Chapter 5

Kids These Daze

Everyone complains about kids, but people keep having them.

No one gets more bad press than teenagers, those nocturnal creatures who trash your house, eat your food, won't pick up their clothes, and generally drive you crazy. Well, they feel the same way about you. Count your blessings. If they felt too comfortable, they'd never leave the nest.

The Graduation Open House Extravaganza

I remember when I graduated from high school, and the events surrounding it were nothing like what we experience today.

To begin with, none of our parents went out and spent a fortune on lavish gifts. In fact, most of us got luggage—as in, "Here's your hat; what's your hurry?"

So, while graduation marks the end of one phase of your life, the term "commencement" refers to the start of something new, like when your parents convert your former bedroom into a family room and pool hall scant hours after you leave for college.

There also is a newly created custom in these parts called "the graduation open house." It appears this is a phenomenon peculiar to the Midwest, as friends of mine on both coasts were completely unaware of its existence.

Anyhow, I'm not sure who created the thing, but it's been picking up momentum for the past 15 or 20 years. The early ones were pretty simple. Dad grilled some burgers and dogs on the old Weber, while mom put out some potato salad and slaw, and the grandparents, nearby relatives, and a few close friends came over to eat lunch and offer congratulations (or "congraduations") to the new graduate.

Since then, the thing has mutated. I've seen wedding receptions that were less complicated.

First, mom and dad either reserve a hall or rent one of those two-acre canopy tents about the size of the Astrodome. Next, there's the food, and the days of Bratwurst and macaroni salad are long gone. Instead, most of these things are being catered, with fancy *hors d'oeuvres,* a complete meal with roast beef and chicken and all the fixings, and a full bar (with paid bartender).

Meanwhile, the new grad, oblivious to the amount of money being spent on this shindig, invites all his family, friends, and relatives, 12 to 15 of his favorite teachers, and every single member of his graduating class (and their guests). This means that mom and dad are dropping enough money to finance a small military operation in order to feed 400 to 500 people.

In return, the guest of honor will be thrilled to receive a few dozen trinkets from his classmates and enough cash to almost cover his first semester's books (none of which will ever be recovered by his parents).

As the parent of a graduate, you will probably receive 20 to 30 invitations to these gala festive occasions (GFOs) and discover that nine of them are on the same day.

So, you'll go to the first one, chow down on beef and chicken and whatnot, and bump into Tim and Sue and Dawn and Harry and everybody else you know in town. As you leave, you'll deposit a nice card with a cash gift on the graduate's display table and head for the next party.

There, you will once again dine on beef and chicken and all that good stuff, and say hi to Tim and Sue and Dawn and Harry and, well, you can see where this is headed. The entire guest list is proceeding counterclockwise from party to party like a slow-moving cattle drive.

By the time you reach GFO No. 8, your checking account is a mere shadow of its former self, while you, on the other hand, are in need of a larger belt. Maybe suspenders.

I'm not sure there's really anything we can do to reel this thing in. The kids are important to us, and we certainly want to wish them well and offer our support. The problem is that I just can't eat that much beef.

So, I have a few suggestions. To begin with, maybe we need a bus to shuttle people from party to party to party. Next, the menus could be coordinated (like a progressive dinner) so you get appetizers at your first stop, salad at the second, a couple of main courses and finally dessert.

Maybe instead we could have the entire graduating class organize a mass party on some large tract of land, like the football field. Each person could set up his or her own display table, and the guests could wander up and down with a roll of twenties, simultaneously eating just one meal and shelling out cash to anyone they recognize.

I look forward to seeing you all at this year's parties, over and over again. I'll be the one with his pants unbuttoned and au jus stains on his shirt.

Helicopter Parents

It's a dark and dismal day.

Little Johnny, an eighth-grader, just discovered the awful grade he received on his term paper. Never mind that it was supposed to be 10 pages, and he wrote only three. Never mind that it was a handwritten mess instead of typed and was loaded with spelling and grammatical errors.

The point is, he got a D (yes, a D) even after skipping part of "American Idol" so he could write the stupid thing, and...

Wait, what's that sound? In the distance, one can hear the steady "whup, whup, whup" of approaching rotors. Is it an attack squadron from, "Apocalypse Now?" No, but you're close. It's Helicopter Parents, here to save the day!

I was gabbing with my good friend M.L. on the phone last evening, and she (a kindergarten teacher in northern Michigan) was telling me about some of the heartburn she has with "helicopter parents."

Apparently, I don't get out much, as I'd never heard the term, but she says it's a new handle for way overly involved moms and dads. The helicopter reference comes from the fact that they hover (loudly) over their spoiled little kids' lives, ready to rescue them from any problem that should befall them. The result is a generation of 30-year-old adolescents who can't fend for themselves.

In the case of poor little Johnny, you can bet that a phone call was immediately made to that rotten excuse for a teacher. And, if justice wasn't restored (i.e., a grade of B or better), subsequent calls were made to the principal, the vice principal, the superintendent, and possibly the pope.

More Abe Lincoln stories: When I was a kid, I was pretty much left on my own (and trusted) to do whatever I wanted, within certain limits. My buddies and I left on our bikes in the early morning. If we were going to be gone all day, we made our own peanut butter sandwiches.

In the course of the day we went swimming without a lifeguard, occasionally fell out of trees, fished in gravel pits, stepped on glass and rusty nails, and sometimes got into heated arguments (or even fistfights) with people we met along the way. If I came home with my clothes ruined, I got chewed out for not being careful.

In school, I was expected to take care of my own problems. I had to manage my own time, study for my tests, and pay the price if I didn't work hard enough. If I'd ever been kicked out of sports for bad grades or gotten hauled out of class by my ear for mouthing off to a teacher, I wouldn't have gone crying to my parents. If I had, my dad would have dragged me into the den by my remaining ear, and I'd have been writing letters of apology to everyone involved (including the pope, and I'm not Catholic).

Today's helicopter parents save their kids from all these pitfalls by intervening in every single aspect of their lives. So, they drive them everywhere, including school, soccer practice, piano lessons, and the mall. There are no overnight stays with friends, as this might create a loss of control. Toss in email and cell phones, and you have a perfect 24/7 tether.

So, every minute of their children's lives is supervised. If a college kid gets caught for illegal parking, mom complains to Public Safety. If the faucet drips in the dorm, she calls the school. If (after discovering fraternities and beer) her boy flunks out, mom threatens legal action and gets him reinstated.

These days, we have "schools of choice." M.L. says she'll get a message that "Abby" will be in her class for a couple of days so her parents can check out the school. She (M.L.) says she feels like she's auditioning for her own job, and wonders what dress to wear, and whether she should submit her résumé to Abby or her parents.

So, how can you tell if you're hovering a bit too much? Apparently, you can find a survey on the Internet, but let's make our own list. You might be a helicopter parent if:

(1) You've called your kid's school more than twice in a week. (I actually received 26 phone calls and emails from one dad in one semester.)

(2) You pay for their speeding tickets and other indiscretions.

(3) Your child is 30, living at home, and you still make his bed and cut the crusts off his bologna sandwiches.

(4) Your child is 30 and still not allowed to go to a sleepover.

(5) You are each No. 1 on each other's speed dials.

(6) He's old enough to be president and still gets an allowance.

(7) You call in sick for him to his college professors. (I had a parent call to explain that his boy missed my test because it was snowing. The problem: He lived 100 yards away in the dorm.)

(8) You visit him once a week—to do his ironing.

(9) You've programmed out the inappropriate channels on his television set—in his apartment, where he lives with his wife.

(10) You don't see anything wrong with Nos. 1–9 above.

The good news is, you'll never lack for company. As long as you keep hovering, they'll keep living with you—forever.

Dorm Pranks

More than 30 years ago, I attended college at Michigan Tech University. It was a rather peculiar place in 1970. The ratio of men to women was about 10-to-1.

Therefore, there was an almost constant droning about the lack of social life on campus. Naturally, the loudest complainers were the ones who bathed and shaved with about the same frequency as they washed their clothes (I've smelled dumpsters that were more fragrant) and had no concept of personal grooming.

To be honest, these guys couldn't have gotten a date on The Island of The Really Lonely Amazons, but I digress. The point is that most of us had to find other ways to entertain ourselves, so we had fishing, skiing, intramural sports, and even (*shudder*) studying.

In addition, we had some interesting people living in the dorms who enjoyed killing time by raising havoc with the other inmates (anyone who says engineers are a bunch of stiffs hasn't met these guys).

While I was there, playing pranks on your neighbor achieved almost cult status. Obviously, we didn't invent the concept. The usual gags, like putting shaving cream in an envelope, leaning a bucket of water up against a door, and ordering pizza in someone else's name had been around since Bonzo was waltzing around with Ronald Reagan.

Our merry band simply decided to take it to the next level (reinforcing the old adage about idle hands). Geniuses they were—Picassos of modern mischief. This analogy was not chosen lightly. You might return to your room to find your potato chips in the shower or your book bag in the toilet.

At about that time, I also recall that cutting classes reached almost epidemic proportions. The faculty probably attributed it to laziness or alcohol use or some of the other usual excuses. In truth, it was paranoia, plain and simple. If you left, your stuff got trashed. The only solution was to stay in your room and protect your inventory like a Doberman guarding a soup bone.

Mine was an old dorm with a lot of play between the wooden doors and the frames. If you pushed really hard, you could insert a penny in the gap, rendering the door almost impossible to open from the inside. Smear a little Vaseline on the inside door handle, and the person was in—for the duration.

We had a guy named Boris who looked like a nerd and had a photographic memory, so we never suspected that he was one of the major pranksters. When we finally discovered the truth, it was like learning Zorro's identity. Naturally, we responded in a most professional and appropriate manner.

He left for class one morning at 8 a.m. and wouldn't be back until lunch. That particular morning it was 6 below, with howling wind and snowing like Nome in January. So, we simply opened his door and his north-facing window. He returned to a big walk-in freezer, with three inches of snow on his bed, floor, desk, books, and everything he owned in the world. They rounded up the usual suspects, but the perpetrator was never identified.

There was a guy named Little Al who liked to have a couple beers on Friday night, after which dynamite couldn't wake him up. It took about three weeks of preparation, including loosening the upper panel on his door to allow access from the outside. Well, Al came in at about 11 on a Friday night and poured himself into the top bunk. He was snoring almost immediately.

It took six of us from midnight until 3 a.m. to fill his room with wadded-up newspaper—flush to the level of his upper bunk bed. I had no idea it would take that much paper to fill a room.

Anyhow, at 8 a.m., we started banging loudly on his door, and Al, who wasn't very tall, swung groggily out of bed and onto the floor, only to discover that he was over his head in yesterday's news. He came thrashing out, laughing and cursing, to find us all waiting in the hall. Afterward, he decided to dispose of the problem by jamming the paper down a third-floor chute that led to the incinerator. Bad idea. The flames emitting from the roof stack looked like a missile launch at Canaveral.

About a week later, the counterweight in the freight elevator (a cast iron ball weighing about 80 pounds) disappeared. Obviously, it was a concern to the custodial staff. However, it surfaced only a few days later.

It was about midnight, and very quiet in the hall, when suddenly there was a rumbling like a minor earthquake. Everyone opened their doors in time to see the world's heaviest bowling ball roll the length of the hall and score a perfect strike, as it liquidated the lower half of the RA's door. We never did find out who was responsible for it.

Speaking of RAs, the most amazing and sinister plan was carried out against the guy a few doors down from mine. His name was Paul, and nobody could stand him. He was constantly reporting people to the Hall Director for the most minor offenses.

I remember a guy named Ray who was a bookworm, rarely left his room, and liked to sip a beer while he did his homework. One night Paul rallied the SWAT team and busted in on poor Ray in the middle of studying for his chemistry final. This act inconvenienced Ray, who was reprimanded for alcohol possession, and elevated Paul to the status of Public Enemy No. 1.

We only got it in bits and pieces, but a commando raid was carried out on the unsuspecting Paul. Dweeb that he was, he always carried his 68 keys on a monstrous keychain attached to the belt loop on the front of his trousers.

So, while he was out, one of Ray's buddies climbed out his third-floor window, shuffled along the ledge to Paul's room, and gained entry. From there, he attached no fewer than six high-tension shock cords from Paul's doorknob to his closet.

An hour later, with everyone in the vicinity peering out from their cracked doors, Paul came whistling blissfully up the hall, inserted his key, turned the lock, and was launched, waist first, into his room at approximately the speed of sound. The force ripped his pants all the way to his knees, but in his anger, he didn't notice.

Anyhow, he came roaring out of the room, shrieking like a Banshee, his pearly white BVDs exposed for all to see. He stepped on the remnants of his right pant leg and went flat on his face. The snickering was so quiet it was deafening.

In retrospect, much of what occurred that year was childish, foolish, and perhaps a bit destructive.

Did I mention fun? Just don't get caught.

I'll Be Home for Christmas

It's almost mid-December and time for Christmas break.

All over the country, moms and dads are eagerly awaiting (and possibly dreading), the triumphant return of their college-age children. Yes, they love them, and of course they've missed them, but there's a certain amount of stress and baggage that seems to accompany the temporary move back into the old homestead and their parents' lives.

First, Christmas vacation is a solid three, count 'em, *three* weeks long. This is (according to college kids) too little time to actually go out, find a job, and earn some real money for spring semester. However, it's way more than adequate for developing a slovenly lifestyle and really getting under your skin.

And so, the prodigal son (or daughter) returns.

He'll enter with a smile on his face, having just completed his final exams, a big hug for mom and dad, and 300 pounds of laundry that he's been stockpiling since Labor Day. Some will be salvageable with copious amounts of Lysol, soap and water, while the more vintage stuff will have to be rerouted to a local Hazmat disposal site.

In anticipation of his return, you'll fuss and prepare a wonderful dinner, complete with cloth napkins, candles, and company china. Afterward, you'll plan to sit around sipping coffee in leisurely fashion; talking about his favorite classes, his impressions of college, the latest on Aunt Martha; and just catching up on the last 15 weeks.

His vision of his first evening back will be somewhat different. Approximately four minutes after arriving, he'll be grabbing some cold pizza from the fridge and heading out to Larry's house, where some of the guys are planning a little party with a couple hundred close friends.

Your first question (still thinking of him as a high school student) will be, "What time will you be home?" This will throw him into a tizzy. He's just spent the last three months handling his own schedule, and a mature adult doesn't have to answer to his parents. He will then confirm this new maturity level by asking if he can borrow a few bucks (just until he's 30) and the family car (just until mid-January).

Thus begins a three-week cycle that will completely throw your well-ordered schedule into the latrine.

College students are nocturnal creatures. They only function at night. If you look carefully, you'll discover that they've developed huge eyes and pallid complexions, resembling a cross between a barn owl and Bela Lugosi. These night creatures eat breakfast at 1 o'clock in the afternoon, have lunch around 7, and sometime during Letterman, as you're cashing in for the evening, will be showering in preparation for going out.

Another problem will be the phone. Not only did your child return home, but 20 to 30 of his old buddies did, as well. These people have no house rules and don't own wristwatches. So, at some excruciatingly late hour, when you're sound asleep and dreaming of sugarplums, the phone will ring, and the kid at the other end won't have a clue as to why you're upset.

Finally, do you remember that neat-as-a-pin bedroom with the freshly vacuumed rug and the matching sheets and comforter? By the third day, it will look like a pipe bomb exploded in a pizzeria. All of his possessions, including his bedding, his clothing (that which could be salvaged), some old, greasy French fries, and the discarded bones from his bucket of chicken will be residing on the floor. In short, it will be an exact replica of his dorm room.

I don't have any good news or words of encouragement. It's like knowing a tsunami is going to hit in two minutes, and there's not a thing you can do about it. All you can do is love them and try to not sweat the small stuff.

In the meantime, cheer up. Summer vacation is only five months away.

May I Have This Dance?

If you can remember when all phones had rotary dials, gas was 29 cents a gallon, and you weren't allowed to wear jeans to school, then you're old enough to remember the high school dance.

I'm not talking about the big, formal types, like the prom and homecoming. I'm talking about the almost-every-Friday-night variety that started after the football or basketball game.

These events were never fancy, but everyone was there. They were always held in the gym or the cafeteria, with a few snacks and a DJ playing records (yes, 45 RPM, vinyl records). And, contrary to its given name, very few of us actually went there to dance. It was just a chance to hang out, watch people, try to fit in with the cool guys, and dream that some popular, pretty girl might show some interest in you.

The chance of this actually happening was as unlikely as a hot Alaskan woman goin' to Washington and livin' in the White House, but that wasn't much of a deterrent. The fun was just in being there. (By the way, that same woman is always goin' huntin' and shootin' elk. It's my theory that her name is actually Paling.)

In a country where all people are supposedly created equal, the high school dance was the classic example of a stratified social class system. There was an elite upper class and, below it, various middle, working, and lower classes.

At the top of the heap were the jocks. They'd make a fashionably late grand entrance following the game, wearing letter sweaters and, with luck, bandaged or taped body parts to showcase the result of some carnage that had occurred on the field. It added to their mystique. These guys hung out in the center of the room, laughed heartily, were revered (or despised) by all, and never made eye contact with lower forms of life. They almost never danced.

At that same level were the really cool girls. They had perfect hair, perfect clothes, and perfect complexions. They weren't smarter or funnier or more talented than anyone else. They also weren't particularly nice, but, for reasons unknown to most of us, they were considered special. They spent an inordinate amount of time in front of the bathroom mirror, glanced around a lot to see if anyone was noticing, and sometimes even danced, but only with the occasional football player who could be pried away from the pack.

The next layer consisted of the upper middle class, as in cool upper classmen. Though not quite elite enough to hang with the BMOC jocks, these people had things that the rest of us lacked and longed for. Specifically, I'm talking girlfriends, sideburns, and their own cars. They were fun to be around, could mix with other classes both above and below theirs, and actually spent most of the evening dancing with their partners.

Next was the lower middle class, as in baby-faced lower classmen. They got all dressed up in pressed slacks, shined shoes, sweater vests, dickies, and after-shave lotion (even though the first arrival of peach fuzz was still months away), hoping to be noticed. Actually, all this attention to wardrobe only increased their Geek Quotients. They huddled in the corner, discussing important issues like chess and trigonometry, and occasionally ventured out to stand near the pack of jocks or ask a senior cheerleader to dance. Fortunately, they handled rejection surprisingly well and usually returned to the safety of their peers very quickly.

At the lowest end was the plain old, nondescript student. He wasn't in any sports or clubs. He didn't have any best friends. So, he flew totally under the radar. He's the guy at your class reunion whose name you don't remember. Anyhow, that night, he arrived after working at the gas station, still wearing his gray working shirt and pants, and sat in the corner, watching the festivities. Half the class probably didn't even know he existed, and the rest didn't care. The irony was that he was probably the only person in the room who couldn't care less what the rest of them thought.

There was another group, mostly hoods and tough-guy bikers who pretty much made their own rules. They had long hair and leather jackets with chains and some logo on the back. They'd come to the dance, but only to make a scene, and soon they'd be thrown out for stirring up trouble. So, at the end of the evening, they'd be waiting in the parking lot, and there was always someone in a fistfight or being hauled downtown by the cops. I'm not sure what level they occupied in the social structure. Actually, I have a pretty good idea, but they might beat me up if I were to share it with you.

The final people in attendance were the teachers, those who drew the short straw and had to ride roughshod on this acne-infested mass of teenagers. Theirs was a thankless task, herding smokers out of the bathroom, breaking up puppy love groping sessions in the dark corners, and keeping a watchful eye out for scuffles and the occasional pint of smuggled hooch.

I've often wondered why weekly high school dances became a thing of the past. I guess I just answered my own question.

Flock is Not a Word

I remember the early days of television, and they don't resemble now.

You'd come home from a hard day at work or school and turn on the tube because you wanted to be transported to an alternative reality where people like Ward Cleaver and Andy Taylor made people's lives a little bit better. It was uplifting.

Back then, there was major censorship by the networks. I doubt you could have said "Hoover Dam" because it contained the "D" word. Do you remember the movie "A Christmas Story"? Poor little Ralphie was overheard dropping the ultimate *faux pas,* the F-bomb. (Hint: "F" does not stand for "faux.") Anyhow, the little twerp had to suck on a bar of soap for his indiscretion.

My, how times have changed. Now we have lovely individuals like Kardashians and Mob Wives and Real Housewives from Mars or someplace who drop F-words at the rate of three per sentence. It's a profanity fest. The network bleeps them out, all the while counting on us to read their collagen-injected lips. Talk about your quality programming.

Speaking of profanity, do you remember Art Linkletter? The man was right: Kids do say the darnedest things. I don't know why it happens, but if a child hears a thousand words, she'll extract the socially unacceptable ones and commit them to memory.

That brings us to today's topic, the one that got Ralphie a mouthful of Lifebuoy. Yes, it's the "F" word. This is a family friendly publication, so we'll hereafter refer to it as "flock."

My granddaughter Alex is 4 years old. She attends a combined preschool and day care and has several teachers. We'll call one of them Miss Jeannetta. Well, she (Alex, not Miss J) came out of the building, hopped into her car seat, and casually said, "Mommy, flock is not a word."

My daughter Amy's eyes got very big, and she figured she had about five seconds to come up with the right response. She said: "Sweetie, who told you that? Was it one of the other kids?" Alex said, "No, it was Miss Jeannetta."

Another panicky long pause to access the internal hard drive, and Amy said, "Why do you think she told you that?" Alex very matter-of-factly replied, "Well, Ryan said 'flock,' and Miss Jeannetta told him that 'flock' is not a word, so we don't say it."

Phew. Actually, it's a pretty savvy response.

If you say nothing, it'll come back to bite you later. If you overreact and make a big deal out of it, the kid will lock on to it like a heat-seeking missile. As a parent, you know that they'll eventually be exposed to this kind of stuff. The goal is damage control. Keep it swept under the rug for as long as possible, and hope it doesn't pop up in church or at grandma's birthday party or some such situation.

If you're looking for some clever words of wisdom or a Dr. Spock-ism on how to deal with unexpected outbursts from your kids or grandkids, I'm as lost as you are. I don't advocate the bar of soap approach; just keep in mind that they are always listening to what you say.

Mostly, I'm just relieved to find out that "flock" isn't a word.

Chapter 6

Boomers

This chapter isn't about thunderstorms. It's about the generation born before television and after World War II, the rebels who brought you long hair, Woodstock, protesting, and Disco (sorry about that one). Nowadays, we just worry about Social Security. Hey, I resemble that remark.

One Man's Trash

There exists in the Midwest a phenomenon so riveting, so ingrained in the cultural fabric of its inhabitants, that many live only for weekends and the chance to experience its intoxicating allure. (Pretty fancy sentence, huh?)

Is it the opera, you ask? No, but nice try.

Perhaps the symphony? A worthy guess but, again, incorrect.

No, this is an event that's more popular than baseball, as American as mom and apple pie.

It's the Yard Sale—proof positive that "one man's trash is another man's…trash."

Every Saturday, after poring over the local papers and plotting strategic travel routes, hundreds of thousands of Americans roll out of bed while the roosters are still sleeping, hurriedly slosh down some coffee and toast, and, like gladiators of ancient Rome, prepare to hit the road and do battle.

The prize, in this case, is a pair of size 24, peach-colored polyester pants with a small spaghetti sauce stain just above the left knee, or perhaps a vintage 8-track player recently salvaged from a 1973 Ford Maverick.

Regardless, it's the Early Bird who gets the worm, or in this case, the mint-green, genuine Naugahyde ottoman.

If you are a yard/garage sale neophyte (I like that word) and considering sorting through your inventory to get rid of unwanted items, take in a little cash, and rescue some floor space, I have a few pointers.

First, the primary reason for the sale is not to make money; that's a side benefit. The only rational reason for giving up an entire warm, beautiful Saturday is that you've found a way to get other people to drive to your house and haul away five tons of unwanted debris.

So, price the stuff for half what it's worth, recognizing that anything you don't sell must be hauled back to the basement. Then, be aware that most of the real yard sale aficionados (I like that word, too) will never pay full price, even if it's 15 cents for an electric can opener.

Next, these people are selective readers. They'll find your article in the paper and easily follow the directions to your front door, but none of them will notice the part about the sale running from 8 a.m. until noon. I promise you that, if it is scheduled to begin at 8, by 6:30 you'll have six cars out front jockeying for pole position.

Then, starting at 6:45 a.m., as you set up tables and begin displaying and pricing your merchandise, you'll have a dozen people pawing through your stuff and generally making it impossible for you to get organized.

Recognizing the dangers, my wife got everything displayed and priced the night before, and had it stored in the garage, away from prying eyes. The plan was to pull all the tables out into the driveway at about 7:55.

On the morning of the sale, she opened the door at about 6:30 to take out the dog and found a woman standing in the driveway, waiting. Jan said, "I'm sorry, the sale doesn't begin until 8." The women gave her a sour look that said, "Try and stop me," walked right past her into our garage, and began rummaging through a pile of children's clothing.

A couple of years later, while browsing through a neighbor's sale, Jan found this really cool, 3-feet-tall, wooden giraffe (every home should have one) for a dandy price. As she was paying for it, a rather nasty woman, who bore a surprising resemblance to the one in our garage, walked up and said, "I saw that first, but I didn't know it was for sale," as though implying that Jan should hand it over. Jan, in a nice way, said something to the effect of, "Well, now you do," and proceeded to her next stop, leaving the woman scowling and sputtering.

My family owns some acreage, and every year we post signs on it to keep unwanted deer hunters out. So, several years ago, I went to my local Kmart or somewhere and found some signs with NO HUNTING written on one side and YARD SALE written on the back.

That's pretty clever, but I recall waking up in a cold sweat one night, positive I'd accidentally tacked it to the tree with the wrong side out. I was sure I'd arrive at the front gate to find 50 irate customers stacked up like cord wood and waiting for the sale to start.

By the way, in a somewhat unrelated sidebar, if you post your property with signs that say NO HUNTING or NO TRESPASSING, it communicates the rules to someone. These days, they have signs that say POSTED. What does that mean? No, really, I'm asking. Bathroom doors are labeled MEN and WOMEN. But if you found two with LABELED on them, which one would you open?

The Good Old Days: Drive-In Movies

As a teenager I (on a fairly regular basis) attended an institution of higher learning that rose up for a brief time and then disappeared into the abyss, much like Atlantis.

It occasionally tries a Lazarus maneuver, resurrecting itself (as in the movie "Twister") to remind us that it's still lurking out there, but most kids these days are completely unaware that it ever existed. To them, it's as foreign as a slide rule or a typewriter or gasoline at 30 cents a gallon.

If you guessed that today's topic is drive-in movies, you'd be right.

The concept was simple enough: A carload of people would drive to this place, park facing the giant screen, hook a speaker to their window, and watch a feature film while eating popcorn and slurping soft drinks.

The commercials always showed a smiling mom and dad in the front seat and two smiling kids (Betty Lou and

Johnny) in the back, sitting politely with their hands folded in their laps like a big, happy Stepford family. Yeah, right.

In reality, no teenager at any drive-in movie theater ever watched the movie. It was just a convenient, dark place for kids to hang out. One boy would borrow his dad's station wagon, and they (the wagons, not the boys) were really big back then. He'd drive to the ticket window and pay for himself and his front seat passenger.

Meanwhile, in the back seat and the luggage area, about 14 of their friends were hidden in a big pile on the floor and under blankets (or in the trunk, if it was a sedan). They'd drive through and park, and it looked like a fire drill as enough people to field a football team piled out.

The window speakers never worked. They chirped and squawked like a flock of demented birds, so most people only watched the movie. I became pretty proficient at reading lips. However, as I said, nonfunctioning speakers were a moot issue, as nobody stayed in their cars, anyway.

There was always a concession stand, which was the focal point of the action. The people there included:

(1) Exotic girls (defined as any girls from any other school).

(2) College students, who seemed so much older and cooler.

(3) Parkers, with partially buttoned shirts, who occasionally left their steamed up cars for refreshments.

(4) Teenage hoods with a pint of hooch and a pack of smokes.

(5) One dad, buying a burger for the family dog in the front seat, and whose kids were asleep in the back seat.

(6) Bikers, with knives and chains and tattoos, who were always looking for someone. It might have been a rival gang member, or the guy who'd beaten up his buddy, or someone who'd hit on his girlfriend, but there was always drama and a score to settle.

(7) One poor security guard trying to maintain the peace.

Not included on the above list was yours truly. I went because my friends did, and I suppose at some subliminal level I hoped I'd meet someone from category No. 1 above. Never mind that I was 16—and looked more like 13—wearing a pressed shirt and sweater vest and looking like a dweeb. Yes, I was the Mayor of Nerdsville, and nobody from category No. 1 was going to notice me, but it was still cool just to be there and check out the people.

Finally, after a couple of fights, several booze confiscations, and three or four crying teenage girls, the unwatched movie would come to a merciful conclusion. The cop would break up any remaining scuffles and eventually usher everyone out.

We'd hit the road and ride around or stop at the Rainbow Grill for a burger and a malt. There, we'd plan next week's trip and talk about how so-and-so had better not show his face, and maybe those cool girls from West Catholic will show up, and blah, blah, blah.

To all you teens out there, sorry. You missed a big slice of American pie.

The Perils of Retirement

As I trundle into my dotage, I periodically run into people I haven't seen for a while, and invariably their first question is whether I've retired.

When I tell them that I'm still working, I usually get a big OMG, followed by a few sarcastic remarks about how being a college teacher is really only a part-time gig, anyway, and we only work 10 or 12 hours a week, and blah, blah, blah.

Anyway, after launching a few jabs at my profession, most go on to regale me with lengthy testimonials about the many virtues of retirement and the chance to finally do all the things I've dreamed of doing.

To me, it sounds suspiciously like, "Misery loves company."

I've heard all the good news about being retired. You're finally free to travel the world. Maybe you'll buy a motorhome the size of the Queen Mary and explore the United States at three miles per gallon, maybe park it in your married son or daughter's driveway, and eat three meals a day with them for a month or so until they finally inquire about how long you might be planning to stay.

Or you can go on a Tour de Old College Buddies and park in <u>their</u> driveways until they finally ask how long you might be planning to stay.

Anyhow, once you buy that $300,000 motorhome and tour in it for a few months, you've not only worn out your welcome in 36 states, but you're out of petty cash, savings, and retirement investments. It's time to head back to the ranch.

This is when the real retirement starts.

The good news is that you have plenty of time to watch daytime TV. The bad news is that you have plenty of time to watch daytime TV. This fact alone scares the bejeebers (I like that word, but my spell check doesn't) out of me. I don't want to spend quality time with Doctor Phil.

I think retirement is potentially a quagmire fraught with peril. You've been married for over 40 years. It was Camelot. Why? It's simple. You left for work at 7:30, did your own thing somewhere else for nine hours, came home, had dinner with your spouse, watched an old movie on TCM, and hit the rack.

Suddenly, you give up working cold turkey. You play golf a couple of times a week, but that's done before lunch. The lawn needs a haircut just once a week. So, you find yourself hanging around the house, spending hours and hours and hours of quality time with someone who has kinda gotten used to having her own space.

After about two weeks of you sidling up to her and asking, "Whatcha doin'?" or "Whatareya planning to fix for lunch?" Arthur and Guinevere are a distant memory, and you're in danger of becoming Frank and Estelle Costanza.

It's time for Plan B.

If you love your spouse and want to stay in your house (very poetic), you should be out from under foot for the lion's share of the day. So, you begin your secondary career as a house painter or a greeter at your local grocery store or even starting your own lawn mowing and plowing business.

How much money you earn is irrelevant, as long as you do it in a different set of spatial coordinates. Don't go away mad…

All of the above is based not on experience, but purely on observation. Maybe I'm wrong. Maybe my bride hopes someday to spend 24 hours of quality time every day with her husband. Maybe we'll both join a Dr. Phil Phan Club. Sure.

All About Singing Turtles

Attention Baby Boomers: I know things are bad. It seems like we woke up one morning and were no longer cool.

We're on the wrong side of middle age. We have male pattern baldness, receding gums, receding savings, bifocals, and a mortgage that's still the size of Wyoming.

We used to think we were going to change the world. Now we're just trying to figure out how to get the kids through college while still holding a little in reserve for when the minivan finally croaks.

Speaking of the kids, they think we're dorks. They don't like our music, our clothes, our friends, or our rules.

Therefore, it is with a heavy heart that I have to tell you this. As it turns out, our lives are a sham, our existence meaningless. We were the Woodstock generation. We lived for the music of The Beatles, The Rolling Stones, Bob Dylan, The James Gang, The Beach Boys, and all those way cool Motown artists. Their lyrics are ingrained in our minds and hearts. We are who we are because of the music of the '60s and '70s.

Unfortunately... oh, how can I tell you this? I've discovered a flaw.

It's in that Turtles favorite, "Happy Together." Hum along, if you like.

"Imagine me and you, I do. I think about you day and night, it's only right, to think about the girl you love, and hold her tight, so happy together. If I should call you up, invest a dime" (A dime? This is where the kids start losing it.), "and you say you belong to me, and etc., etc."

Stop humming. After all that double negative stuff where I can't see me lovin' nobody but you, and baby the sky will be blue for all my life…

Here it comes, the dreaded line (drum roll please):

> "The only one ***for me is you, and you for me,*** so happy together."

Rats. Did you catch it? We have prepositional dysfunction.

The only one *for me* is you, and you *for me*. It says the same thing twice. Both times it's you for me. There is never anyone for you. You might as well be a hermit living in a line shack in rural Alaska, because you are nowhere in the picture.

I can see the blood draining from your faces.

You're stunned, shattered, the very fabric of your zit-faced teenage existence ripped apart at the seams. It would be like finding out that John Wayne was actually a tall-in-the-saddle transvestite. (No, no, don't panic; he wasn't.)

I wish I had some words of consolation for you, but I don't. It's a little late in the game to abandon everything we held sacred and start over searching for the meaning of life.

My suggestion is to take two aspirin, put on a Peter, Paul and Mary album, dig out your old bellbottoms, feel as groovy as you can, and comfort yourself in the knowledge that you're really embarrassing the kids.

Chapter 7

Potpourri and Stuff

This chapter is just a big gunnysack filled with unrelated nonsense. We'll call it "potpourri," because that sounds sweeter and more fragrant than "other crap."

The Rebound Barber

Most of us have agonized through the loss of important people in our lives. And no, this isn't going to be a maudlin discussion about losing parents and grandparents and spouses.

I suffered through something even more gut-wrenching. Yes, I lost my barber.

Scoff if you will, but craftsmen (and craftswomen) of hair are as rare as passenger pigeons and skilled surgeons. Most of us go a lifetime without finding that one, true coiffeuse. (Cool word, huh?)

However, thanks to a stroke of good fortune, I came across Brenda. The woman was a master. She always gave me the perfect cut: artfully tapered, skillfully trimmed, and leaving enough bangs to not further accentuate my more than ample forehead.

Ours was not an intellectual or emotional relationship. I suppose you could say that it was purely physical. It was an outpatient procedure.

I sat in the chair with my mouth shut while she snapped gum next to my ear and conversed with the other stylists about her boyfriend coming home late from the bar or what was on sale at Walmart. It was quite fascinating. In addition to the perfect haircut, I was privy to some pretty valuable inside information.

But, to paraphrase Geoffrey Chaucer, all good things must come to split ends, and so it was with Brenda. She up and vamoosed one day without so much as a "Later, gator."

Naturally, I was devastated. For a while, I went into seclusion. My hair, left unattended, left me looking like Arlo Guthrie (but without the musical talent). Finally, unable to see, I decided it was time to rejoin society.

I went through a series of rebound barbers, but they were just one-day stands. Honestly, I don't even remember their names. After several of them, I finally settled on a transitional relationship. She was pleasant, and the haircuts were of decent quality, but it wasn't the same.

The magic just wasn't there.

Anyhow, I was pretty much resolved to the fact that I would never have it that good again, when I stopped in for an appointment and found out that my regular girl had called in sick. Plus, all the others were booked.

On a whim, I decided to try a new place, and that's when I found the greatest barber since Figaro. We'll call her Denise.

Anyhow, life is once again a bowl of cherries. (I have no idea what that means.) Regardless, thanks to Denise, I can again count on the perfect haircut every time. She not only has a good sense of humor, but she's a super mom and grandma, and the bonus is that she doesn't snap gum in my ear.

I haven't broached the subject with her yet, but she has to work for at least another 20 years, and she's not allowed to move. I'm not going through this again. I hope she understands.

Wimps of the Universe

As a faithful follower of CNN, "Unsolved Mysteries," and "My Favorite Martian," and as a big fan of science fiction movies new and old, I've become increasingly aware that planet Earth must have a monstrous "KICK ME" sign taped to its back (probably somewhere in Australia).

You may have asked yourself how it is that one little chunk of spinning rock in one little solar system in one little galaxy can attract every alien within a million trillion light-years of here.

Well, I believe I have the answer.

Hard as it is to admit, I believe we are the dweebiest 97-pound weaklings in the universe and that aliens from every corner of space actually plan long weekends and use vacation time just to come here and kick sand in our faces.

We have to start training, people! Somehow, we have to get smarter, stronger, faster, and savvier if we want to survive.

These aliens come in two basic categories.

The first (as in "The Day the Earth Stood Still") are the benevolent, fatherly types (the space-age version of Ward Cleaver) dressed in aluminum-foil spacesuits, speaking impeccable English, vastly more intelligent than we are, and here on a peaceful mission to save humankind from its evil ways.

We usually respond to this show of kindness by firing Howitzers at them.

The second group appears to be incredibly angry about something (perhaps their in-flight movies were old episodes of "Lost in Space") and are always here in search of human blood.

What's with that? Haven't they tried the sirloin steak or grilled shrimp, or perhaps the barbecued ribs?

Anyway, we initially ignore the obvious problems (pods lying about and Uncle Jack, who never blinks and now speaks in a slow monotone) until it's too late, and then we again (futilely) fire Howitzers at them.

We went through a big surge of these invasions back in the '50s, and then people began to get a little complacent as the number of encounters dwindled and the problem seemed to disappear.

I'm not so sure. Remember the classic movie "The Thing"?

The space creature (a vegetable man who could regenerate himself) was cut out of the ice, brought back to base, accidentally thawed out with an electric blanket, and finally destroyed by the members of the arctic outpost, who used an electrical current to dispatch him.

Well, I don't think he's *really* dead.

Is it coincidental that the creature bears a very strong resemblance to Marshal Matt Dillon? I think he's still out there, hanging out at the Long Branch with Kitty and Festus and just biding his time.

I'm also concerned that some of these aliens may have aspirations of getting into politics.

In "Predator," you might recall that the title character was an alien hunter who stalked through the jungle in search of human skulls for his trophy case.

Not only did he take out Apollo Creed and a gaggle of his ultra-macho friends, but he also managed to kill the governor of Minnesota and nearly dispatched the governor of California, who finally managed to outwit the ugly dude by dropping a log on his (the alien's) head.

This raises the question of who might be next, and is this nasty creature a liberal or a conservative?

My hope is that, somewhere in the universe, there's an entire race of aliens who are smaller, weaker, and less intelligent than we are. Then, as they roll out of their spaceships, bent on destroying the human race, we can mop them up like a tribe of Pee-wee Hermans.

Because this isn't likely, I suggest that you start lifting weights, studying astrophysics, and maybe dusting off the old Howitzer.

Meanwhile, keep watching the skies!

Chickens Don't Belch (or I'll be Culling You)

I have good news for all you gas-guzzling enthusiasts out there who want to ride around in pickup trucks the size of Sherman tanks, burning fossil fuels at the rate of three gallons per mile.

As it turns out, your vehicles' emissions are only a portion of the problem. A huge part of the global warming issue is actually attributable to the methane produced by belching cows.

No, really. I read it, so it must be true.

Everyone just naturally figured that the billions of tons of carbon emissions produced by cars, trucks, power stations, and factories were the primary cause of all our problems.

However, bovine burp is made up of methane and nitrous oxide, which are 21 times and 310 times, respectively, more effective at trapping heat than carbon monoxide is. No wonder the polar ice cap looks like an ice cream cone in August.

Believe it or not, in a scientific study, France discovered that its 20 million cows account for 6.5 percent of its total greenhouse gas emissions. Plus, cows account for 80 percent of total animal emissions, so pigs ain't the problem.

However, the bad news is that bovine flatulence is negligible when it comes to global warming. In English, this means that the big problem is the northern end of a north-bound cow. Too bad it's not the southern end, or we could simply manufacture a few million corks and solve the global warming crisis.

OK, we've identified the issue, but how do we fix it?

The articles I read suggested all sorts of dietary changes, such as different grasses and clovers, or perhaps higher-protein fodder. There were also innovative approaches, such as pills or vaccines to reduce methane production. I'm thinking that industrial strength Maalox might do the trick.

However, the simplest approach would be to simply reduce the size of the world's cow herd. With fewer cows you get less gas. Duh.

The concept sounds easy enough, but somehow we have to first reduce their numbers and then get the world's beef eaters to switch to soy milk and poultry. After all, chickens don't belch. They're leaner and lower in cholesterol, and, well, they taste like chicken.

So, how do we reduce the number of cows in the world and the corresponding tons of greenhouse gases? The quick fix would be to cull the herd by 25 percent. My suggestion, to deal with the carnage, would be to create a World Barbecue Day, with a gigantic feast of steaks, short ribs, and baked potatoes for the entire planet.

Unfortunately, this concept is not being universally accepted. Basically, the cows are up in arms, er, hooves over the whole idea. A spokesbovine (Bessie) for the SPCC (Society for Prevention of Cruelty to Cattle) noted that in some regions of the world (those like India, which practice Hinduism) the cow is a sacred animal.

Though she's not expecting royal treatment or a radical religious revolt on the part of the entire planet, she suggests a gentler (and much less tasty) approach to the reduction of bovine numbers. In the same way that we reduce the number of upper-management positions in a top-heavy company, she suggests that herd reduction could be accomplished by not, uh, replacing individuals as they "retire."

More unfortunately, her proposal is not being happily embraced by the world's bull population. After all, their primary functions are chasing drunken idiots down the streets of Pamplona and making little cows. In short, there will be little need for their services in the foreseeable future, so they may become expendable.

If I were a bull, I think I'd head for India.

Barbie's Midlife Crisis

There are some people—like Liz Taylor, Madonna, and Julia Roberts—that you expect to get married and divorced about as often as you change your oil, and other couples that you just naturally assume are paired for life, like a couple of Canada geese.

That's why it came as such a shock to me when I heard on the radio that Barbie and Ken had split up. No, really.

According to the news report, something like 2 million people completed a survey suggesting who her next main squeeze should be. As a result, little miss 5-foot-11, 104 pounds, with certain body parts that simply must have been enhanced, has ditched her longtime beau and has been spotted running around with an Australian surfer named Blaine.

The whole thing reads like a cheap tabloid.

Perhaps I shouldn't be critical, since the power of the midlife crisis can lay waste to even the strongest of marriages, but I can't see this thing being any more than a short-term fling.

First, I know she still looks good, but does Blaine really have any idea how old she is? I mean, the woman is over 50! Sure, she still looks good, but that's only because, very much like Cher, the majority of her body parts are plastic.

Plus, it's not like she ditched Ken for a good provider who could put a roof over her head and give her everything she needs. The guy's a surfer, for heaven's sake, a Down Under, overly tanned beach bum with a funny accent, six-pack abs, flowing blond hair, and no ambition to do anything except hang out, hang 10, and search for the perfect wave.

Sure, it may be romantic and exciting for a while, but 10 years from now, when she's applying for Social Security, he's going to ditch her like a plate of leftovers.

And what about the guy who's really getting hurt by all this? Poor Ken has to be devastated.

OK, I know he's not perfect. First, he isn't anatomically correct, and that certainly is a major consideration.

Plus, he's pretty quiet and a little stiff, but what Midwestern Caucasian male isn't?

Let's consider his positive attributes. First, he's still exceptionally handsome for a guy his age. It's not as though he's a troll or some freaky looking Cabbage Patch doll. (My niece had one whose name was Crystal Georgiana, but she was so ugly they called her Crystal Drano.) Plus, he's been totally devoted to her for all these years. Shouldn't that count for something?

Mark my words, this thing isn't over. Before too long I'm predicting she'll be back on her hands and knees (if they bend, that is), begging his forgiveness.

Even more worrisome is what this says about the crazy state of this world we're living in. If Barbie and Ken are going the way of Liz and Dick, what's next? I suppose we'll be hearing that Nell is dumping Dudley Do-Right and hooking up with Snidely Whiplash, or maybe that June Cleaver has run off with Fred Rutherford.

It's almost more than a body can handle.

Big Brother Is Watching

Big Brother just moved into my building.

It happened subtly enough. There were guys with tools and stepladders milling around, and I just figured that we were having heating or cooling issues. Not so.

When I walked in the next day, the walls and ceilings were adorned with a myriad (I like that word) one-eyed spyware devices normally associated with casinos. We are not alone.

I understand the reason for it. We have a lot of computers and other valuable equipment hanging around this place, and we don't want it wandering off.

However, having this many electronic hall monitors can be rather disconcerting. Who is on the other end? Are they watching our every move? Is my job in jeopardy? Do these pants make my rear end look big?

It's interesting to see the effect that this addition has had on our resident employees. It's like some weird behavioral experiment.

Some people apparently feel intimidated, so they walk by with their heads lowered, avoiding eye contact with the thing. Others are putting on sport coats and getting their hair styled like they're going to an audition. A few Type A personalities find it offensive and either snarl or give a one-fingered salute as they pass.

Regardless, it's affected us all.

My biggest issue is the weight gain. I've been eating a lot of salads and fat-free yogurt to get in shape for biking and running this summer.

You know what they say about the camera putting 10 pounds on you, right? No? Well, they say the camera puts 10 pounds on you.

Anyhow, every time I walk down my hallway, I've got two of these contraptions tracking my every move. That's 20 pounds of extra lard I have to haul around. I'll never get into those biking shorts.

The other big issue is hackers. You've heard about what happened to the patrons at Target. Millions of people had their personal data compromised. What if the Russians get tired of watching Sarah Palin and decide to tap into our network? What if they see me in the hallway? Will they understand about the 20 pounds?

Another bothersome thing I've heard, and it may be just a rumor, is that Santa Claus may use this electronic monitoring technology to develop a worldwide Naughty and Nice spreadsheet.

As Ray Stevens said, "He's everywhere, he's everywhere."

There won't be any reason to appeal, because your indiscretions will be right there on film for Santa and the Russians and everyone else to behold. I just hope you like coal.

I'd like to continue this little article, but I hear that J.C. Penney is having a sale on size 58 pants, and I want to stock up before they run out.

Just remember that you aren't paranoid. They really are watching you.

Velvet-Tongued Car Sales

Hey, buying a car is a pretty big deal these days. Your basic SUV costs more than I spent for my first house, and we're likely to keep the things longer than the average marriage.

Therefore, we all want the best fit and the lowest price. Unfortunately, many of us are genuinely fearful of setting foot on the lot and being accosted by an over-eager salesman.

To salesmen everywhere: All we want is the straight scoop. I've met a few car salesmen in my life who actually give you the straight line, and the approach works wonders.

The last time I bought a car was from my friend (we'll call him Don). I drove to the lot, took a vehicle out for a spin, liked how it handled, and asked about price. Don showed me the Blue Book value, told me the boss would price it at $21,500 but might settle as low as $20,500. I offered $20,000, whereby he countered at $20,250, we shook hands, and I left

30 minutes after walking into the place. Unfortunately, guys like Don are pretty scarce.

To all the non-Dons out there, there are two sales methods that really bother us and actually cause us to take our business elsewhere.

The first we'll refer to as "The Tight Squeeze Blue Book Scam."

I decided to look for a new car, but had one to trade. So, before leaving the house I called the bank and got a Blue Book range on my present car. They told me it had a $5,300 average trade value and $7,500 average retail.

When I got to the dealer, I was admiring a new car and was latched onto by Tight Squeeze Phil. He asked me if I was in the market, and I told him that it depended on what my trade was worth. He examined my car, produced his book from his buttoned shirt pocket, and, clutching it tightly, opened it about a sixteenth of an inch, periodically glancing up to be sure I wasn't trying to peek.

"I'll give you $2,800," he said.

I laughed and suggested that he must be mistaken, whereupon he again cracked open the book and said, "Nope, that's what it's worth."

Then I did a crazy thing: I asked to *see* the book.

From the look on his face, you'd have thought I'd just confessed to the Lindbergh kidnapping. He got all flushed and started stammering. I'll bet he had signed an oath to eat the thing rather than let it fall into enemy hands. Anyhow, I got sick of trying and finally just left.

The second way to turn us completely off is by using "The Tag Team Method."

I was ready to start negotiating on a car but unfortunately was given to the greenest salesman in the place. His name was John, and he looked about 12, and he'd obviously just passed CS 101 (Intro to Car Sales).

His car listed at $19,000, and mine booked at $8,000, an $11,000 difference. I figured to trim a bit off his profit margin and hoped to get the car for mine plus $10,000. (That seems reasonable, doesn't it?) The problem was that everything had to be run through Frank, the unseen tag team partner.

John started things out by saying, "Bob, you're really in luck, Bob, because Frank is really feeling generous today, Bob."

I asked how generous, and John Boy wrote a number on a piece of paper and pushed it over to me, his face beaming. The paper said, "$14,000." Swell. I told him he wasn't even close. He looked heartbroken.

"Well, Bob," he said, "What do we have to do, Bob, to put you in this car, Bob?" I suggested he lower the price about four grand. "Just a minute," he said. "I'll go talk to Frank."

Ten minutes later he returned, after negotiating fiercely on my behalf with the alleged Frank, and produced another piece of paper with "$13,700" written on it. Hot dog, now we were getting somewhere. I tried the rational approach, explaining that I wanted the $8,000 average trade for my car, and I wanted his for $18,000. He narrowed his eyes suspiciously and said, "If you want me to lower my price, then you have to lower yours."

Hoo-boy. I tried once more to explain that if we each lower our prices by a thousand bucks, the difference doesn't change. This only seemed to confuse him, so I finally asked to speak directly to Frank. He said he'd see.

Five minutes later he returned, not with Frank (whom I was now convinced was his invisible little friend), but with another piece of paper, which he again pushed across to me.

"Bob," he said, "Frank can tell you mean business, Bob, so he's decided to really give you a deal, Bob." I looked at the paper, which had "$13,500" written on it. I suddenly remembered some urgent business I had to attend to, and I said I'd call.

I never went near the place again, Bob, but I'm tempted to drop in some time and ask for Frank.

Have You Seen Your Squatch Today?

As January slowly ticks to a close, and we've endured almost two weeks of nonstop Super Bowl pre-game blather, I find myself seeking anything as an alternative (well, except for the Kardashians).

Some of the stuff on Animal Planet is pretty cool. There's a show called "River Monsters," in which the host,

Jeremy Wade, travels all over the world in search of the biggest and toothiest. The guy's a rock star. Not only does he endure some pretty nasty conditions, but he also usually lands the fish.

On the same channel, at the opposite end of the quality spectrum, is a show dedicated to finding the elusive (or nonexistent) Bigfoot.

Oh, man, what a great scam. I only wish I'd thought of it first. The network set out to assemble a team of cutting-edge research scientists, but couldn't find any on eBay, so they dug up four gullible fraternity brothers who enjoy wandering around in the woods.

The head of this merry band is a glassy-eyed dude who reminds me of an acquaintance (Larry) from college. As I recall, he had a close and personal relationship with a certain weed.

TV show Larry is a man who sees a Sasquatch lurking behind every rock and tree.

Every episode has the same plot. The team is outfitted with all kinds of high-tech surveillance equipment, audio recording devices, night vision goggles, and cool stuff like that. They toss in a couple of cases of beer and some beef jerky and set off for some remote location purportedly (I like that word) teeming—yes, *teeming*—with Sasquatches.

There they meet some of the locals, many of whom actually agree to take time away from Dr. Phil to tell their stories. Most have breathtaking, near-miss accounts of their close encounters with the big, hairy beast (Bigfoot, not Dr. Phil).

Following these interviews, they drive to a remote corner of the remote location and set up camp where several Bigfoots (or is it Bigfeet?) have been sighted. While this is going on, Larry loves to tell us that "this place is really squatchy looking, and the perfect place for a sighting."

Of course, he's never actually seen one, but that doesn't diminish his enthusiasm.

So, they first go to the exact place where some local guy named Gus claims he saw a Squatch. Gus stands on the road, and Larry walks a hundred paces into the trees and stands exactly where Gus says the alleged ape-man was watching him.

Then (this is the scientific part), Larry asks Gus if the thing he saw was larger or smaller than he (Larry) was. Naturally, Gus says it was way taller than Larry and didn't look anything like a black bear. With that they conclude, beyond a shadow of a doubt, that it was eight feet tall and definitely a Bigfoot.

And you were skeptical.

Then, they all spend the night in tents, and something goes crashing through the bushes, and something else makes a loud moaning sound (possibly one of them falling into the latrine), and they go scurrying around in the woods with their goggles on, so everything is green and spooky.

Finally, as the episode is reaching its climactic finish, one of them sees a pair of green eyes peering at him through the murky haze, and just as the tension is so thick you could cut it with a knife, suddenly, emerging from the mist—drum roll… more drum roll—nothing happens.

That's right. Nothing.

In the end, they all just go home. They have no hair samples, no droppings, no sightings, no plaster footprints, nothing. They didn't see squat, er, Squatch. And yet, for reasons unexplainable, they're already into Season Six.

I think I'll start my own outdoor reality TV show. Every week, we'll visit another Michigan county and search for the elusive white rhino.

We'll title it "Gullible's Travels."

You Can Call Me Alphonse

It's bread and water and turning big rocks into small rocks for yours truly. I'm headed for the slammer, the clink, the cooler, the stockade, the Big House (no, not the one in Ann Arbor).

I got the call early Saturday morning, so I let the answering machine pick up. On the other end was Steve Martin. It didn't sound like the banjo-playing comedy star of stage and screen.

This Steve Martin had a nondescript Sydney Greenstreet sort of accent. He may have been from Russia, or possibly France, or maybe even northern Ohio. At any rate, his message said he was a representative of the U.S. Treasury Department, and this was my third and final notice regarding an income tax problem from 2012. I was told that I would have to take care of it immediately or face punitive (I like that word) legal action.

What a nice way to start the weekend.

So, I checked the number, and it supposedly originated from California. That seemed a little odd, since it would have been 4:30 a.m. on the West Coast. I called back, and it was answered by some woman who had apparently taken a three-day intensive English course from Elmer Fudd. Press "1" if you want to hear this message in broken English.

After 30 seconds, it was pretty obvious that this was all a scam, but I had nothing better to do.

Well, she really launched into it. "You have dewinquent tax wetoon from 2012. It appeaws dat it was just mistake. You must wectify pwobwem immediatewy. If you do not, wepwe-sentatives fwom waw enfocement weo come to yo home and awest you and take you to fedewa pwison. Do you want to go to fedewa pwison?"

I told her that I already had weekend plans and didn't really want to go to fedewa pwison. But, since both my daughters live in Kansas, I asked if she could arrange to have me sent to Leavenworth (a gated community). That way, I'd at least have plenty of visitors.

She started getting frustrated with me, so I kept piling it on. I said, "So, if you can just tell me what part of my tax return is in error, I'll talk to my accountant and have him investigate it."

Sensing that she was no longer in charge, she decided to ramp up her threats.

"You do not have time to contact tax accountant. If you do not pay dewinquent taxes immediatewy, waw enfocement wiw come to yo home in Big Wapids. Dey wiw awest you and put handcuff on you in fwont of yo famiwy, and dey will take you to fedewa pwison."

Wow, I guess when hardened criminals like Al Capone and Bob Eastley get nailed for income tax evasion, it's right to the front of the line, buddy. Go directly to jail. Do not pass "Go." Do not go to court. Do not collect $200.

I should have stopped, but this was too much fun. I said, "Elmer, I'd like to give you my bank account and credit card numbers to settle this issue, but I'm having trouble understanding your English. Could I please speak with your manager?"

She put me on hold for two minutes and then came back, pretending to be someone else. "Who awe you twying to weach?" I said, "I'm not trying to reach anyone. You called me. I'm just twying, uh, trying to stay out of federal prison."

She took one more shot.

"So, you awe wiwing to give me cwedit cod numba? I said, "No, I promised to give that to Elmer. Could you put her back on?" She put me on hold again, and that's when I hung up. They haven't called back. Go figure.

Don't get scammed. If they call, ask for Elmer.

CPSIA information can be obtained
at www.ICGtesting.com
Printed in the USA
LVOW04s1127060716
495317LV00017B/186/P

9 781945 37958